HIDDEN H

WITNE<< MEN

True Stories of God at Work in Papua, Indonesia

WHAT CHILDREN ARE SAYING ABOUT HIDDEN HEROES

This is my favorite Christian book!

I'm thinking of being a missionary myself!

This is probably the best missionary story I've heard.

I love your books! They're really good!

You've really taught me a lot with these books!

It's perfect.

The chapters all have great names!

These are the best books ever!

I love your book please write more books I love them!

I have learned to be a better testimony!

I want to hear more!

Hidden Heroes 1: *With Two Hands:*
Stories of God at Work in Ethiopia

Hidden Heroes 2: *The Good News Must Go Out:*
Stories of God at Work in the Central African Republic

Hidden Heroes 3: *Witness Men:*
True Stories of God at Work in Papua, Indonesia

WITNESS MEN

True Stories of God at Work in Papua, Indonesia

REBECCA DAVIS

CF4·K

10 9 8 7 6 5 4 3 2 1
© Copyright 2013 Rebecca Davis
ISBN: 978-1-84550-972-9

Published in 2013
by
Christian Focus Publications,
Geanies House, Fearn, Tain,
Ross-shire, IV20 1TW,
Great Britain

Cover design by Daniel van Straaten
Cover illustration by Fred Apps
Other illustrations by Fred Apps
Printed and bound by Nørhaven, Denmark

To the missionaries of Dutch New Guinea; West Irian; Irian Jaya; West Papua; and Papua, Indonesia (all the same place!) who have taught me so much and shown Christ to me. I praise God that I have the privilege of giving a small picture of your story for children.

To access more information and activities about
Witness Men, see the Christian Focus website at

www.christianfocus.com

Contents

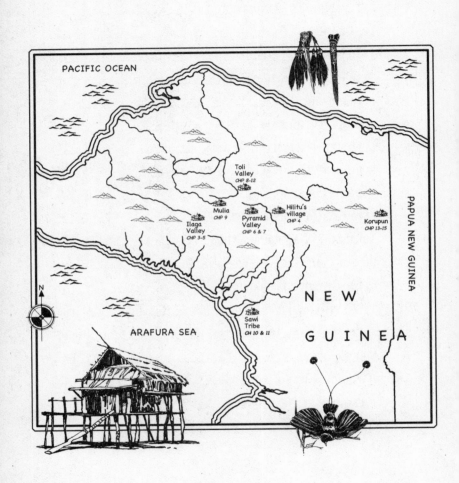

PACIFIC OCEAN

Toli
Valley
CHP 8-12

Mulia
CHP 9

Hilitu's
village
CHP 4

Korupun
CHP 13-15

Ilaga
Valley
CHP 3-5

Pyramid
Valley
CHP 6 & 7

PAPUA NEW GUINEA

N

NEW

Sawi
Tribe
CH 10 & 11

GUINEA

ARAFURA SEA

I NEED TO EXPLAIN SOMETHING ...

Several things, actually. And they're all about names.

For one thing, the name of the book. Really, there were Witness Women too, and they were very important, mainly the missionaries' wives and the single ladies who came. But the book is primarily named after the men of Papua who took the gospel from their own tribe to other tribes. And it really was mainly men who did that. The missionaries called their training places "Witness Schools," and the men who learned there were "Witness Men."

I need to explain the name of the place, too. The large island above Australia is divided into two parts. The eastern half is called Papua, New Guinea, but that's not the one this book is about. The western half was for years called Dutch (or Netherlands) New Guinea. Then its name was West Irian. Then for years it was called Irian Jaya. Then it was called West Papua. Now it's called Papua, Indonesia, but its name might change again.

There are also names of several tribes, small or large groups of people who all lived in the same land: the Damals, the Danis, the Sawis, and the Kimyals are only a few of them. They have some similar customs, but very different languages, sort of like the Americans and the Germans, or the British and the Polish.

Sometimes I simplified the names of the Papuan people, so that reading the book wouldn't get discouraging. Their real names are in the back.

Finally, you're going to see several missionaries' names in this book, not just one. So many of them came to the very same area—dozens, even hundreds of them over the course of a few decades, all descending on a land about the size of Nebraska—that I decided not to limit this story to just one. In the back of the book I tell more about who they are and when they worked in Papua. Several of these pioneers have been kind enough to correspond with me.

And there's one more Name I want to talk about: the Name of Jesus Christ. That one Name is the reason for people giving their lives, for all the rescue from darkness and sin and fear, and for all the praise being offered from shore to shore of the land of Papua, Indonesia.

1. DISCOVERY!

Through white clouds and above a foaming river the airplane coasted, over the high mountains, tall as the Rockies. But these mountains weren't rocky. They were covered with forests and jungles, streams flowing down, raging rivers rushing around and through. It was Dutch New Guinea.

"What in the world…." The explorer, Richard Archbold, held the binoculars to his eyes. "I can't believe it. Russ, do you see what I see?"

The pilot squinted out the window and nodded. Below them, in the huge valley along the river, lay small tan circles that could be nothing except grass-roofed huts. "I see them," he said. "It's not your imagination. Those are houses, all right."

Richard let out a long, slow whistle. "They'll never believe this back in New York. They will never believe it. Who would've ever thought there was a valley this huge in the middle of all these mountains? That there are *people* living here?"

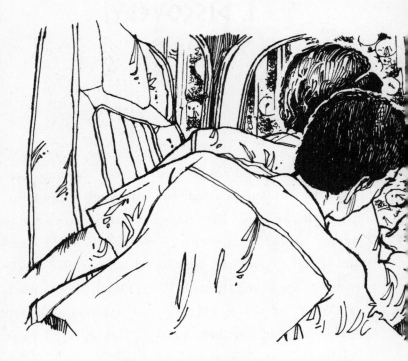

"How many do you think?" Russ asked. "Looks like hundreds of them."

"Thousands, I'd say," came the reply. "And if there's a family in every one, then maybe fifty, sixty thousand people."

All the other dozens of men in the exploring party also strained their eyes out the windows of the airplane. "Look, can you see the stone walls?" one of them asked.

"I can see the outlines of all the gardens. Looks like New England farmlands!"

"This was supposed to be an *uninhabited* territory," Richard muttered.

While the explorers marveled, down below the tribal people were reacting too. They stared up at the giant silver bird in the sky, crying out with fear or awe, cowering or wondering or threatening. Some of them had heard that such wonders existed, but almost none of them had ever seen one.

It was 1938.

These were the Dani people, only one group of what turned out to be hundreds of thousands of tribal people in Dutch New Guinea, discovered by the outside world for the first time.

And neither the Danis nor any of the other tribes had ever, through all the centuries of their existence, ever dreamed that any outside world even existed. Through all their generations they had thought they were the only people. The only people in the world.

Their world was about to undergo a gigantic change.

See Thinking Further for Chapter 1 on page 139.

2. ACROSS THE WORLD

The photo up on the big screen showed a dark-skinned man with a bone stuck through a hole in his nose, his long black hair hanging down his back in a net.

"Yes, they really do look like this." The white-haired speaker, Mr. Ebenezer Vine, scanned the faces of the hundreds of students at Prairie Bible Institute. "But we know that the magazines are wrong. These tribes aren't 'a last look at our evolutionary ancestors.' They're people like us, made in the image of God, who need the gospel just like we all do."

As Dave Scovill and his future wife Esther gazed at photo after photo of Dutch New Guinea, a father of the Western Danis showed his son the best way to throw a spear in order to kill a man quickly.

"These tribes live in constant fear—they don't know anything else. Yes, they're afraid of each other—they get into tribal wars at the drop of a hat, or of a pig bone. When they're in a feud, they'll kill anybody they

see from the other clan. Doesn't matter if it's an old person or a child."

As John Dekker and his future wife Helen listened intently, the Dani warriors of the Toli Valley stalked into a neighboring village to strike down women while they fed their pigs and men while they dug their gardens.

"Imagine never knowing whether you or your loved ones would even live through the day." Mr. Vine showed a photo of a dark-skinned face with fear-filled eyes. "But, you know, their fear of each other isn't even their worst fear. Their worst fear is fear of the spirit world. These tribes don't worship spirits—we don't think they even have a word for worship. But they're constantly trying to appease the spirits—performing secret rituals and public ceremonies to keep the spirits from troubling them." He showed a photo of a human skull. "They hope that the skulls of their ancestors will give them special strength. They offer pigs in sacrifice. They say certain words. They don't say certain words. They cut off fingers. They might even offer their children. They hate the spirits, but the spirits control them. They don't know any other way."

And while David Martin and his future wife Margy listened, someone in the Toli Valley Dani tribe was killing a woman he feared to be a witch.

17

"You can see that these people wear almost no clothes. Their customs are strange. They keep all these strange little items—fetishes, charms—that they think will give them special power." He showed pictures of shells and bones and weapons and skulls. "Some of the things they do will turn your stomach. Some of them are cannibals."

As Don Richardson and his future wife Carol listened, people of the Sawi tribe were butchering the body of a man they had just killed.

"Students, I want to tell you a story." Mr. Vine stopped and leaned his hands on the podium, focusing his eyes on first one face and then another. "It was just a year ago, in February of 1954, some missionaries went in to this valley area."

He gestured toward a map of New Guinea. "They were the first white men this Dani tribe had ever seen. The Dani men—they'll kill you as soon as look at you—they came out with their huge spears, their bows and arrows. But, listen to me, students. An old man, the witch doctor leader of the tribe—picture him almost naked and his body slathered all over with pig grease—he came up to these missionaries weeping. He threw his arms around them. Can you picture that missionary getting that pig grease all over himself?"

The quiet auditorium rustled with a murmur of laughter.

"What was that old man saying? Why was he crying? Were his people just waiting for the gospel of Jesus Christ?"

Mr. Vine gripped the podium. "But the missionaries had a problem. They didn't know the language, so they couldn't understand him. Even now, as I speak to you, they're still trying to decipher it, so they can give the gospel to these people—remember, they are people like us, people that Christ died for!—to give them the gospel in the Name of our Savior who died for them."

And as the students listened, new missionaries were heading out from all over, to new tribes with unfamiliar languages, trekking through underbrush that required hours to cut through, undertaking the long hard job of building airplane landing strips in the jungle.

"It will be difficult," Mr. Vine said. He showed a photo of those impossibly huge mountains, the same mountains the explorers had flown over seventeen years earlier. "If we're going to take the gospel to these tribes, first we have to find them. Some of them are hidden away in valleys we don't even know about yet. You'll have to trek for days to find them. You'll have to clear land for the airstrips before you can even bring in your wives and children. You'll have to learn a language you've never heard before." He scanned the crowd, his penetrating eyes piercing.

"They may fear you, they may misunderstand you, they may hate you, they may even kill you. But they need the gospel, and we must go. We must go!"

As Phil and Phyliss Masters leaned forward and prayed, someone in the remote Kimyal tribe cried out in a long, low wail over the hopeless death of a loved one.

While each of these future missionaries, and many others, spent the next years studying and preparing and learning and praying, through the tribes were stirring whispers of old, old legends.

While some of the missionaries studied in language school, an old Dani chief in his clan's man hut reminded his sons that one day someone would come, a pale man, over the mountains, one who had discovered the secret of nabelan kabelan—forever life.

While some missionaries were learning how to fly the mission airplanes, an old leader of the Damal tribe was dying, murmuring to his son, "Maybe in your lifetime the mysterious stranger will come, bringing the golden age of hai, the perfect paradise on earth. My son, keep watching for hai."

While missionaries studied nursing, anthropology or mechanics, around a fire in the remote Kimyal tribe a man once again repeated the legend that a ghostly person would come one day, dressed in spider webs, to teach the way of life forever.

And a Kimyal boy named Siud gazed up at the jagged mountain peaks. He had never been taught about any sort of God at all, but he knew there must be something more than the spirit world his witch doctor father taught him. "I won't become a witch doctor," he murmured. "There must be a greater Spirit, and one day I'll learn about Him. There must be a Spirit who loves."

When the missionaries boarded airplanes that would take them to Indonesia and then to Dutch New Guinea, a young Dani tossed in his sleep, dreaming that someday a man would come who would give them ki wone, a word of life. Then he dreamed that he himself would teach these strangers the Dani language.

And while the missionaries on the island's coast prepared to trek to remote inland regions, a man from the Sawi tribe with tears handed his very own child to another tribe in order to bring an end to a long war, to make peace. If only this peace child could live forever.

One by one, two by two, witness men and witness women came from all over the world, to tell those who walked in darkness that there is Light ... to give the Living Words ... to explain the secrets of eternal life ... and to lead them to the one Peace Child who really did live forever.

See Thinking Further for Chapter 2 on page 139.

3. THE GOLDEN AGE OF HAI

Chief Den sat up in the darkness in a cold sweat. He was having that dream again.

Gripping his arms, he rocked his body back and forth, moaning softly. Next to him, one of the other men stirred. Quietly Den got up and stepped over the bodies of the sleeping men and boys to climb out. The air outside was heavy, but clearer than the hazy smoke that always filled the man hut.

"I am chief," he muttered. "I shouldn't be afraid. But I'm always filled with fear."

He leaned against a tree and closed his eyes, moaning.

It had been so many days since his cousin died, a cousin that he loved like a brother. How could he bear it? The agony tore at his stomach, day after day.

He sighed heavily, remembering the journey he had taken over the mountains, to village after village, asking all the witch doctors to tell them what had happened to this man who was like a brother. Where was he in the spirit world? What was the purpose of his death? No one could tell him. Only a few days ago Chief Den had returned home, with no answers.

He reached out into the darkness and clutched his fingers around nothing. He shuddered and gripped his arms again.

When morning dawned, the chief was still leaning against the tree. The people of his tribe began emerging from their huts to begin the work of the day. The women fed the pigs and tended their sweet potato gardens, the men took their spears to go hunting. Muttering under their breaths, the people chanted words that were supposed to ward off the angry spirits. Some men stationed themselves at the edge of the village to watch for warriors from the neighboring clans, with whom they were always at war. They knew that the men of nearby villages loved to swoop down and grab people out of their gardens and kill them.

Den groaned in his soul. "O my father," he muttered. "When you died you said that I might see hai. You had all those dreams about hai. But the only dreams I have are about darkness that never ends."

Den tried to remember the beautiful dream his father had described to him before his death, a dream that seemed to be a picture of the beautiful golden age that the Damal people longed for. A shimmering tree that gave him sweet fruit when he was dying of hunger. A pure sparkling fountain that quenched his great thirst.

"My son," his father had said. "Hai will bring a new world for our people. All my life I have searched for it. But our ancestors tell us that it will come suddenly, and it will come in a strange way, a new way. I could not find hai by searching. It must find us. Perhaps in your life, you will welcome spirit beings who will bring hai."

Through the years Chief Den's people, the Damal people, had told the stories around the fire. Their stories told about the golden age of beautiful long life, of fat pigs and plentiful gardens, no war, no sickness, no fear. They imagined all the glory that their small world would allow.

O friend, up in the sky is a big boat on a great lake,
Ah-wai-wai. Ah-wai-wai.
And to this wonderful place we want to go.
Ah-wai-wai. Ah-wai-wai.

Then they would grow silent, wistfully dreaming of a life that seemed impossible.

But Den's dreams had become more than wistful. He was desperate.

It was only a few days later that Den's son Nogom stood before him. "Father," he said. "Spirit beings have come to the Ilaga Valley. Tuans."

25

Den's eyes became large with wonder and fear, and he felt the hair on his arm stand on end. "Tuans? Have you seen them?"

"No, Father. But I talked with others who saw them. They have pale skin, like the spirit beings I saw when I traveled far. They wear coverings that are made by spirits. A spirit bird drops things to them out of the sky."

"Find them!" cried Den. "Find them and bring them here!"

Nogom set out immediately for the village where two men, Don Gibbons and Gordon Larson, had come a few days before. Not knowing the language, they couldn't tell these people that for five days they had been slogging through soggy marshes, scrambling over rocky cliffs, trudging through freezing rain, simply to arrive here with the good news of the great God who loved them and sent His Son to die for them. They couldn't tell these people that they had been preparing for years for the work they were starting now.

The Damal people watched their every move. Nogom stood and watched them too. Then he took a deep breath and stepped forward. "Greetings!" he said in Indonesian.

Don looked up from his work. "You speak Indonesian?" he asked, incredulous. It was a language he understood!

"Yes, a little," answered Nogom, slowly, carefully. "I have traveled far. I have known other tuans."

Don almost trembled with excitement. *Thank you, Lord! We can communicate!*

"My father is a great chief of another village," Nogom went on. "He wants you to come."

As quickly as possible Don prepared for the trek with the young man. He marveled at God's great work that allowed him to communicate immediately with the people in this remote jungle.

As they hiked from one village to the other, Don saw the dark-skinned faces behind the trees, behind the huts, watching, watching. Usually with fear, but sometimes with shy smiles.

Back and forth in front of the man hut Den was pacing, when a runner came to him to tell him that the tuan was coming. Den put on his feather headdress and his largest necklaces of cowrie shells.

There came the tuan. So tall! So much bigger than the Damal people! So pale, like the dead! And covered with a covering that must be from a different world.

Den was ready. He was ready for the message of hai.

He walked forward with a quiet dignity, different from other loud, boasting chiefs. "I am Den," he said simply. "I welcome you." Nogom translated his words. Den stretched out his hand and snapped his fingers with the pale man again and again to show his greeting. "I want you to live in my village," he said. "I have a place where you can build your house."

After building small huts, Don and Gordon offered the people cowrie shells and steel axes for helping them flatten an area of land for an airstrip. Eagerly the Damals came and worked, delighted with the cowrie shells they earned, amazed by the steel axes that could chop down a tree in just an hour.

But after a few days had passed, Don held up his hands. He held up finger after finger, until he had reached seven. "On this day," he said, pointing to finger number one, "we will stop work. That is tomorrow. You will come and listen to me teach."

Nogom translated for the people. But no one understood. A day has a number? What kind of tuan talk was this?

"It is the day of rest and teaching," Don said.

The next day, instead of preparing to work, Don stood outside with his Bible, waiting for the people to gather. When the Damals found out they wouldn't be paid, only a few came. But Den was one of them.

"We are men," said Don, "but we bring a message from the Greatest Spirit." He pointed to the sky. "He is greater than all the spirits of the earth. He is over all, over all spirits, over all men." Don waved his arms to form a large arch. "He made all men. He made you, and He made us. He is the Great Maker."

Chief Den looked up in the sky. He contemplated this Greatest of all Spirits, who had such power, to make tuans who looked so strange, and to make real people too. *I don't want to miss hai when it comes. Are these tuans bringing hai?*

Day after day the Damals worked on the airstrip with Don and Gordon, digging up grass and rocks, moving loads of mud, dumping loads of sand, smoothing with their hands. Earning their beautiful cowrie shells.

Night after night the men of the village sat up in the man hut, stringing their cowrie shells and trying to figure out what these tuans were doing. Now, they no longer talked about how to plan the next battle with their enemies or how to keep the spirits away. Instead, they talked about the tuan's words. *What did he mean? Could it be true? Was he bringing hai?*

"People are bad. We all do bad things," Don taught. "But the Great Maker has great love. He has a Son who came to die for the sins of all bad people, so that we can become good people and live in His love. He came to give us forever life."

Murmurs went through the crowd. *Is it hai?*

The airstrip was finished, and the frightening airplane arrived. With it came Don's wife Alice and their two daughters. They would live here among the Damal people while Gordon went on to another tribe.

Don continued to preach. Don and Alice continued to pray.

And Chief Den continued to listen and wonder. *Are my people being given their long-lost hope?*

But Nogom, the chief's son, the translator who listened and spoke the words of the gospel day after day, was the one who first came to Christ. When he gave his steel axe to a man from whom he had stolen a pig, everyone in the valley knew Christianity had changed him. "Did you hear? Did you hear what Nogom did? Is this hai?"

After some days had passed, a man came from a tribe on the coast. Widi-abi traveled all over the land with the gospel. "This news that the pale men give you is true!" he said. "It's true for tuans, and it's true for real people too! It's true for my people over the mountains,

31

and for the Damal people, and for all the tribes! Jesus Christ is the God of love, the God of eternal life!"

After that, hundreds and hundreds of Damal people gathered to listen to Don Gibbons preach. The men stayed up late at night, talking and talking. Would their tribe accept this new message? Finally, a day came when Den called the other Damal leaders.

"My people," he said. "Our ancestors have waited for hai for many suns. My father waited all his life for hai, but he never saw it.

"But now these strange tuans have come from the other side of the mountain. They have spoken good words to us about the Great Maker, who is so great that He can make all things, even real people and tuans. They have told me about this Great Maker's holy Law. We know that we have broken the Maker's holy Law. This is why we live in fear. But there is a great Rescuer, Jesus Christ."

The other chiefs sat in silence, eyes wide, as Den closed his eyes and raised his hands. "These words are hai! We must believe them so we can have hai once more! This is the fulfillment of our long, long hope!"

See Thinking Further for Chapter 3 on page 139.

4. POWER PIECES

The boy called. "Tuan Botemon!"

Tom Bozeman came out of his little house to see the bright-eyed boy. Tom had lived here among this Dani tribe a few months, and had learned enough words to begin teaching the people a little bit.

"Greetings!" he said, snapping his fingers with the boy's. "I remember you. You're Hilitu, yes?"

"Yes," the boy said. "I talked to you at the cannibal feast yesterday."

Tom's face turned a little bit green at the memory. "I should never have gone to that. I didn't believe it would really happen. That wasn't good. That was bad."

Hilitu shrugged. "It may not be your way, but it is our way. It's how we show the enemy we hate them. When we capture a warrior, we get his power pieces and we—"

"Yes, yes, please," Tom Bozeman interrupted, putting up a hand. "I do remember you. I'm glad you came, Hilitu. How can I help you?"

The boy smiled broadly. "I want to be your helper, here, at your house," he said. "I want to live here."

"But don't you have a family?" Tom shaded his eyes and gazed out beyond the airstrip at the huts, watching the dark bodies moving around in the fields. They looked so peaceful compared to the wild partying and screaming from the night before. "You can't leave your father."

"Oh, no, Tuan," Hilitu answered, smiling. "My father was killed in a battle, and my mother—my mother just died." He shrugged.

"Who do you live with?"

"My brother, my uncle. But they won't care if I live with you. They'll be glad for me to be gone."

"Well, I have to say, I would be very thankful to have a helper living here." Tom opened the bamboo door to his house. "Fran! Here's the little boy I told you about! He wants to come be a helper for us."

Frances Bozeman came from the other room of the house with her two little children. "Wonderful!" she cried. "Hello, young man!"

Hilitu reached out his grease-covered hand and shyly touched the foot of the baby that Fran was carrying. "Tuan Botemon," he said, shaking his head, "faded babies are so surprising."

Tom built a small house for Hilitu to live in, next to the missionaries' house. Fran started a class to teach

Hilitu, along with several other boys, how to read their own language. Every day the boys stared at the strange markings on the white sheet as Fran explained the sounds they were supposed to make.

Hilitu learned quickly, and before long, he was reading simple stories.

Weeks passed. Every Sunday Tom stood outside his house and preached in the native language, as well as he could. But only a few people would listen, and most of them didn't seem to care.

"There is a Great Maker!" he cried out. "He made you, and you, and you, and He made me!"

"That's foreign talk," one man muttered.

"Our chief will kill us if we believe you," said another.

But Hilitu sat with bright eyes, listening closely.

Through each week, Tom helped the people and tried to learn their language better. Every Sunday, in spite of the discouraging response of the people, he preached. "The Great Maker sees the wrong we do. He says, 'No!' No bad things can come before Him. But the Great Maker loves people, all people, and He made a way for people to become good."

"We don't know any Great Maker," muttered one man. "We know only the spirits. We don't want to come to them. We just want to keep them away."

"Foreign tuan!" cried another. "You've come to try to trick us! You'll make the spirits angry!"

But through the weeks as Hilitu studied the words of his language, as he helped Tom and Fran give medicine to his people, he watched and listened. "This sore skin, Hilitu, see?" said Tom, helping a sick man who had come to their door. "This is yaws. I have healing liquid for this." He pulled out of his bag a needle and drew up some medicine into it. Then he injected it into the man. He prayed in the Dani language, "Great Maker, this man has a sore body. You are the Great Maker, and You are the Great Healer. O, Maker, you love this man. Touch him and make him well." Hilitu listened and wondered.

A few days later the man's skin began to heal. "This is spirit work!" the people whispered to each other. "This tuan has powerful spirit liquid."

"No," said Hilitu, "this is helping liquid from the Great Maker. The tuan calls it medicine."

But one day a man that Tom tried to help didn't get better. When he died, he cried out, "I'm burning!"

Tom touched his head and felt the fever. But Hilitu was frightened. "Tuan," he said, "you talked about the great good place of the Maker you call heaven, and you talked about the great dark place of fire you call hell. My people say that when you die, your spirit will sink down below the earth, with the ghosts. What is true?"

Tom didn't have enough words. How could he tell people about sin and grace and salvation when there were no words in their language for those ideas?

So Tom did the best he could. He crouched down the way the Danis do when they have an important meeting. "Hilitu," he said, "You know I talk to the Great Maker." Hilitu nodded, his eyes large. "I have been talking to him about you. I say, 'O Great Maker, help Hilitu to understand and know.' Now I want to tell you something. My son, you know that your people always have fear?"

Hilitu nodded. "We're afraid all the time. So many things are forbidden. If you step in the wrong place or you touch the wrong thing or you say the wrong word. Then the spirits will get you and eat out your insides. Or make your skin rot. Or make your pigs die. Or make your babies die. Maybe a witch has put a curse on you, or—"

"Yes, yes," said Tom. "You understand about all that. But I want you to understand about the true God, who can take away fear."

Hilitu's eyes grew large. "My people say that's impossible, Tuan. They say you're crazy. We'll always have fear!"

"But I'm serious." Tom lowered his voice and spoke with a sense of urgency. "The true Maker, the only truly Good Spirit, the greatest Spirit who is over all the other spirits, He can take away all fear, because He is so powerful, and He is so good."

Hilitu folded his arms. "These are good words you speak, Tuan. Living without fear ... huh. That's something my people need."

Fran kept working with Hilitu to teach him to read. Before long he was reading and understanding Bible stories in his own language. When he listened to Tom preach, his eyes were bright.

"The Greatest Spirit, our God, is very far above us!" Tom said. "But because of love, Jesus came to make a way to get to the Great Maker. He died. Then He got new life. He gives that new life to all who come to Him."

Weeks passed. No one seemed to be listening.

Except one small boy.

"I want this Jesus," Hilitu said one day. "I want Him to give His medicine to me here." He touched his stomach. "O Jesus!" he prayed. "Take away all the bad things I have done. I steal things. I eat people. I lie."

Tom watched Hilitu's eyes fill with tears as he prayed. "I want you and Mama to teach me about Jesus all the time, Tuan Botemon," he said. "I want to live without fear."

As Tom worked on repairing the airstrip for the airplane or took medicine to the sick people or helped his family, Hilitu was often at his side. As they worked,

Tom taught. Hilitu learned about an entirely different spirit world than the one he had known before.

One day, as Hilitu was helping Tom carry a heavy load of dirt, he stopped and looked up at the sky. "I have no fear," he said. "I want to talk to the Greatest Spirit for the men who killed my father."

That night he came to Tom and Fran with a net bag. "Look, Tuan," he said. From the bag he pulled out a pile of what looked like trash. Bones, stones, arrows, feathers, something that looked like string.

"What are these?" Tom asked.

"Oh, Tuan, you don't know?" Hilitu arranged the small pieces on the floor. "These are my kuguwak. My power pieces. These are the special things that give us connection with the spirit world. Only men can look at them. If the women see them, they have to die."

Hilitu held up a bloody arrow. "See, this came out of my father's body. I kept it to give me power against my father's enemy. And this ..." he held up the string-looking thing. "This is a pig's gut. It's to help pigs grow strong and fat. This stone is to keep evil spirits away from the garden." On and on he went, describing how each useless-looking trinket was supposed to accomplish something in the spirit world.

Magic charms, thought Tom. *Fetishes.*

Then, very abruptly, Hilitu gathered all the pieces into a heap. "But I came here to tell you that I'm all done with these kuguwak. They're weak—they're part of the bad spirit world. And they're part of our fear. Now I know that all power comes from the true God, the good Spirit, the Great Maker of heaven and earth and men and animals. I don't want to try to get power from anywhere else. I'm going to throw all these power pieces into the river."

Tom walked with Hilitu to the edge of the river and watched him throw all the pieces in. As they sank down and swirled out of sight, Hilitu prayed, "Lord Jesus! You've taken my fear! You've given me strong insides! Now I no longer hold my power pieces! Now I hold You!"

The story spread throughout the Dani tribes—"Hilitu has destroyed his kuguwak! Hilitu prays to the tuan Spirit! Hilitu won't work on the tuan rest day! Hilitu won't fight in our wars!"

One day, as Tom and Hilitu trekked together up a craggy mountain, Hilitu stopped at the ridge and looked down. There he could see his people, the Dani people, below. He stopped and lifted his hands. "Lord Jesus!" he prayed. "You've given Your good medicine to my stomach. My people need Your good medicine too. Give it to them, so they can be free from fear."

And Tom looked down and said, "Amen."

See Thinking Further for Chapter 4 on page 140.

5. NABELAN KABELAN?

A chief called out to Gordon Larson, "Tuan! Welcome back."

It was 1958, and Gordon Larson had just returned from the United States to the Dani people of the Ilaga Valley, where he was continuing to teach, to build, and to help the people. The Dani men, who were big and strong, were glad to help him build an airstrip for his airplane. In exchange, Gordon gave them beautiful cowrie shells and amazing steel axes.

"I'm glad to be back, Lalok," Gordon answered. "What is your news?"

Lalok stood tall and strong, his long gray hair hanging down his back in a net bag. "Do you remember that before you went away, my son-in-law found hai?"

"Yes, I remember your son-in-law," said Gordon. "He's Den of the Damal tribe. He came to Christ just before I left."

"Before you went away, Den's people burned their kuguwak. All the Danis in the Valley knew about it."

"I remember," said Gordon. "Another chief told me that all of you would be watching the Damals. He wanted to know if their pigs would die or their gardens would fail, or if their babies would die or their enemies would kill them."

"Yes, I said that too." Lalok shook his head vigorously, and his net bag swung up and down. "But for these many suns, the Damal people have not suffered at the hands of the angry spirits. They have been kept safe. Truly, the Damals have found hai. Tuan, all the Danis are talking about it." He swept his arm across the air in front of him to show how far the astonishing news had traveled, like shock waves through one valley after another.

"But your people haven't received our preaching," Gordon reminded Lalok. "You think that no spirit can have love, that no spirit can be good. You think that no man can rise from the dead."

"Yes." Lalok nodded slowly. "But the Damal have searched for hai for many seasons. I know that my son-in-law is not a fool. If he and his people burned their power pieces and have suffered no harm, it is because they found something even more powerful. Come over here to the grass behind these bushes."

Gordon squatted down with Lalok. "Tell me more," Lalok whispered. "Who is this Jesus you talk about?"

"He's the Great Maker who became a man like us," Gordon said, repeating words he had spoken many times. "He's the Great Spirit come to earth because of love."

"My son-in-law says that this Jesus will give life that goes on and on," Lalok said anxiously. "Will my son-in-law live forever?"

"He won't live forever on this earth, but after this life, he'll have eternal life with the great God, Jehovah. That's because Den no longer holds to his power pieces, but he looks to Jesus only for his power."

"So maybe this is the nabelan kabelan of the Dani," said Lalok.

"Tell me about nabelan kabelan," said Gordon.

"The bird dies, of course. But the snake lives forever, as we can see by the new skin he gets again and again. Long ago the snake and the bird had a race, and the bird won the race. Our ancestors foolishly followed the bird and lost the way to live forever. But we believe that someday we will again find nabelan kabelan, "my skin your skin." That is the forever life that our ancestors lost. Then we will have no more death, no more fear, no more hard work, no more war. Maybe what you tell me is this."

"I can't promise no more hard work. I can't promise that you won't die. But I can promise that in Jesus

Christ you can have no fear. I can promise that in Jesus Christ you no longer have to have these terrible wars. I can promise that in Jesus Christ you can live forever after death."

But Lalok still looked anxious. "If we burn our kuguwak, will our pigs die? Will our enemies win battles over us and kill us?"

"You must be ready to trust Jesus Christ, to know that He is true," said Gordon. "You must believe in Him alone. But He can give you freedom from your fear."

One day Lalok came to Gordon and said, "See this?" He held up a handful of shell necklaces. "These are the cowrie shells of my father's father. If I burn these, I fear that I will have no power in battle. My enemies will kill me and destroy my people."

"Then wait," said Gordon. "Our God is very great. Greater than all the enemies, greater than all the power pieces of the world. You can put all your faith in Him for all your power. When you're ready to do that, you'll want to burn your kuguwak."

47

Lalok gazed up over the high, high mountains. "I want my people to be free from the power of the spirits," he murmured. He shook his head, and his long matted braids swished back and forth. "But I can't burn my kuguwak unless all my clan does it with me. We do all things together. That is our way. Maybe next month we'll have a burning." He looked at the cowrie shells, and his shoulders sagged. "These things are like strong vines around us, but we're afraid to burn them. We want them because they help us have power, but really the spirits use them to hold power over us."

Over the days and weeks and months, Lalok and the other leaders continued to ask questions and listen. Now they listened with open hearts. The Damals had found hai. Would the Danis miss nabelan kabelan?

One night, the time had finally come. Lalok sat with Gordon alone in the man hut. "I will burn my kuguwak," he said. "I will look to Jesus Christ. He will protect me. My power pieces will not." He took a deep breath, and his lips became set in a firm line. "If the other Dani clans don't want to join me in the burning, I'll do it anyway."

"My people!" Lalok announced to his village the next day. "We cannot learn about the true and living way until we cut the strong vines that bind us, like the Damals did. These kuguwak are strong vines binding us to the spirits of fear!"

Was it right? The people felt the tremor of fear shiver through their bodies. Was it right? Would the spirits be angry?

"My people!" Lalok repeated. "We must do this. We must burn our kuguwak to be ready to receive nabelan kabelan."

The leader of the clan had said it. They were a people together.

So it was that the next day, on the outskirts of the village near the airstrip, people gathered sticks for a huge fire. Then, some with joy, some with fear, brought their power pieces, in piles and bags.

The flames leaped up and caught the kuguwak. Brightly the fires burned and burned and burned.

The Danis of Lalok's village had burned their power pieces. And the news of those flames traveled like a forest fire through one village after another after another.

See Thinking Further for Chapter 5 on page 140.

6. JABONEP THE WITNESS MAN

The teenage boys of the Dani tribe in the Pyramid Valley jumped and shouted outside the missionary's house with such energy that their hair bags bounced on their backs. "Tuan Yon! Tuan Yon!"

Henry Young got out of bed and came to the door, where he could see the sun just beginning to peek over the horizon.

"Tuan Yon, you must hear! In another village, near us, a man has come who can't see. He is very short. The gun shot him many years ago. It went right through him, but he's still alive!"

"What? What are you talking about?" Henry Young passed his hand over his sleepy eyes.

"Long times past, this blind man went away, but now he has come back! The river! The river waters stop and let him go by on dry ground!"

"Who is it?" Henry asked. "Where did you get this story?"

"Didn't you hear about him?" one boy insisted. "If he dies, his family won't burn him. They'll just throw him in the river. Then he'll *come back to life!*"

All the boys sucked in their breaths, their eyes wide.

"And then we'll be able to see the spirits of the dead, Tuan!" another boy added. "They'll look like you!" But the boys were too excited to laugh. They nearly trembled at the wonder of this amazing man. "Do you want to come see him?"

"You'd better believe I do," Henry muttered. He got his clothes on and walked with the boys to the nearby village. They continued to chatter all the way.

From a distance they could see the crowd. *How many here?* Henry wondered. *Must be thousands.* They were still gathering, coming from villages all around. Everyone was chattering about the amazing stories they had heard.

There was the man! But hmmm. It wasn't one man; it was three. And none of them were blind.

"You boys got your stories a little mixed up," Henry said. "None of these men look like the man you were talking about."

The boys smiled and shrugged and nudged their way into the crowd to listen. They didn't care that stories could get twisted as they traveled from village to village.

The man who appeared to be the main speaker came up to Henry. "I am Jabonep," he said. "I am from the Witness School in Ilaga. I want to give these people the gospel."

"Well, I wish you success," said Henry. "I've been preaching it for years, but they don't show any interest."

More and more people gathered, jostling each other as they sat down in the center of the large village. The other two witness men and others with loud voices, stood here and there throughout the crowd.

And so the "echo preaching" began.

Jabonep lifted his hands to the sky and turned his face upward. "Greetings, our Maker, greetings!" he said.

The echo preachers near him copied his actions and his words. Then other men here and there throughout the crowd did the same. "Greetings, our Maker, greetings!"

Once the echo system started, it moved very quickly. Every line was echoed, echoed throughout the crowd, to make sure everyone could hear, even the ones farthest away.

"Today we are here! And the tuan is with us!"

"The tuan knows about You and what You have done for us!"

"He has told these people about You, but they have not listened!"

"So we have come to tell them about You and about Your words."

"We have heard Your words, so we no longer follow the old bad ways."

"You have given Your good Spirit to us, our Maker!"

"You are good, and You are enough, our Maker!"

"You have given Your knowledge to the tuan!"

"I am all done talking with You, our Maker!"

"Your eyes are like the shining stars."

Jabonep opened his eyes and looked at the people and began to preach.

"There was a blind man!" Through the thousands of people his preaching was echoed again and again.

"He could see nothing!"

"But there was a man—Jesus!"

"He had great power!"

"Jesus touched the eyes of the blind man ... and he could see!" Jabonep popped his hands together and apart and then stopped, while everyone gasped.

Henry Young looked around at the crowd, and saw that all of their eyes were as big as seashells. Especially those teenage boys who had come with him.

"That man Jesus was not a man like us!"

"That man Jesus was not a man like the tuan!"

"That man Jesus could walk on the water!"

Once again everyone in the crowd gasped.

"That man Jesus was the Son of the Great Maker!"

All eyes were riveted on the preachers.

"They killed that man Jesus! They put a spear right through him!"

Well, that isn't exactly right, Henry thought.

"But that man Jesus came back to life! He lived forever!"

Henry could hear the whole crowd breathe in awe. Then they began whispering to each other so fast that he couldn't even understand what anybody was saying.

Jabonep waited. When he spoke again, he directed his hand at one person after another.

"You are bad! You are bad!"

"You steal pigs! You kill people! You eat people! You speak not truth!"

I've been telling them that for years, Henry thought, *but they just laugh at me. They think I'm talking like a crazy tuan. And they keep stealing my tools.*

"You are turned toward the bad spirits!" Jabonep continued.

"But that man Jesus can make you turn to the good Spirit!"

Suddenly Jabonep cried out, "Put your head down on your knees!"

As Henry watched in amazement, everyone did! *I've never been able to get them to do that.*

Jabonep again lifted his hands to the sky and turned his face upward.

"Great Maker!" Through the crowd echoed the words. "Great Maker! Great Maker!"

"You look down at these people!"

"Give Your spirit to these people!"

"Give your words to these people!"

"You are great, O Great Maker!"

"Your arms stretch across the land."

"I am all done talking with You now."

When Jabonep finished, the people stood up, soberly, quietly. Some whispered, some didn't speak at all. There was far too much to think about.

And Jabonep and his friends went on his way.

The next morning, several of the Pyramid Danis came to Henry Young's house.

"Tuan Yon!" they cried. "We want to listen to your words!"

When Henry walked out, he saw some of his tools that had been missing for months. "Where did those come from?" he asked.

"Somebody took them, Tuan," said a man earnestly. "But somebody brought them back."

"Huh," Henry muttered. "Wonder who that somebody was. But it looks like the gospel is making a difference."

Henry turned to another man. "Why didn't you listen to me all this time when I was preaching? What did Jabonep do different?"

"Tuan, your words were foreign words. When we heard that witness man, we knew those words were from our own people. They were for us. So now we want to hear your words too."

Through the days as Henry preached, more and more people came. "We heard the witness man! We want to hear more of the Jesus words!"

One day, one of the mightiest leaders in the area came. "Jesus has repaired my heart!" he cried out. "I want you to teach my wives and my children!"

Another old man who had hated the missionary said, "I am a Christian now! I will go to heaven with you!"

So many people were coming to Christ, so many people wanted to be taught, that Henry Young asked for more missionaries and more witness men to come to help him.

Over six thousand people came to listen to the echo preaching.

See Thinking Further for Chapter 6 on page 140.

7. BURNING THE POWER PIECES

Jim Sunda shouted to his wife over the two-way radio, "You're going to have to get back here to Pyramid right away!" They're going to have a burning, and it's going to be the biggest burning yet! I don't want you to miss it!" The Sundas had been in Pyramid Valley with the Youngs only about six months, but already exciting things were happening.

"We're going to burn our kuguwak!" The Dani people of Pyramid Valley couldn't contain their excitement and fear at this decision that they knew would change their lives.

They began to gather sticks for the burn pile. A huge pile, to make the greatest bonfire any of them had ever seen. It stretched twenty, thirty, forty feet long, three feet high and six feet wide.

"The Pyramid Danis are burning their kuguwak!" The message traveled through the surrounding villages as quickly as if the people were using telephones. Damals and other Danis from the Ilaga Valley, clans who had already burned their power pieces, jumped with joy. "We were praying for our enemies!" the Damal Christians exclaimed. "And now they're having a burning!"

The Christian Damals came. The Christian Danis came. Deloris Sunda arrived to stand with her husband Jim, holding their newborn baby. Other missionaries and their children came. Other Dani people came, just to watch and wonder.

As the visitors arrived on the morning of the burning, almost all the people of Pyramid Valley began to pour out of their huts. The ground pounded in rhythm with the drumming of their feet. The men and boys ran to the spirit huts that held their power pieces. They pulled out old bloody arrows, ancient strings of cowrie shells, nets full of pig tails, and knives carved out of bone. "Today we burn the old ways!" one old man shouted. They grabbed the objects that they had thought sacred and stuffed them into their net bags. "Today we find freedom from the spirits!"

More and more people brought their kuguwak. Some carried net bags filled with dozens of them. Strangely shaped stones, pig fat, pig guts. Wands made of bright bird feathers that they had waved in the air to try to keep the spirits away. The nets became so full that they stretched almost to the breaking point.

Hundreds and hundreds of people came with their power pieces. More and more and more. Then it was thousands. Thousands and thousands. Over eight thousand people of the Pyramid Valley brought their power pieces to burn. They ran down the trails to the airstrip, singing and shouting, and piled their net bags high on the mountain of firewood.

For this greatest ceremony in their history, the men had carefully decorated their faces and bodies with bright red and white clay, along with soot mixed with pig fat that glistened in the heat. Feathers and impressive head pieces adorned their long hair.

The men began to gather in groups. Then they began to circle around each other, in and out, in and out, in a ceremonial dance to celebrate this grand event. The women moved in circles around the circles of men. A chant rose from a low murmur, louder and louder.

Then an old leader held up a torch. "We burn the fire today!" he cried. "Today we burn away the old spirit world!" He set the torch down to catch fire on one stick. It caught another and another and another.

The people cheered and clapped and stomped, in rhythm with the flames. "We want heaven! We want eternal life!" they cried.

"Keep no kuguwak!" one leader cried. "Burn them all!"

"We want heaven!" the people chanted. "We want nabelan kabelan."

"You women!" called another leader. "Hold no kuguwak! No witchcraft!"

Some women still looked fearful, but others replied with the chant, "We want heaven! We want Jesus!"

An old witch doctor stood up, raising before the crowd an old dried piece of meat and cried out, "I am done with this old life! I want heaven!"

The people danced and stomped their feet as the flames grew higher and higher, licking up the kuguwak that had held them in bondage to the spirits.

"We're free from our old ways!" someone cried. "We're free!"

The chant moved around and around the huge circle as people from more and more villages came to watch. "We're free! We're free!"

A voice of an old leader stopped them. "What have we done today?" he asked. "We've cut the strong vines to the spirit world. We've opened the way to learn about the Great Maker and His great Son Jesus."

"The Great Maker has more power than the spirits!" another shouted. "We can learn about Him and his power! We're no longer in bondage!"

"We're free! We're free!" the people echoed.

And the dancing continued long into the night as the fire burned and burned and burned.

Before a year was over, more than twenty clans had burned their power pieces. Then over the next two years there were more ... and more ... and more ... until many thousands of people—eventually even Hilitu's village—had built great fires to take the first step in breaking from the spirit world and finding freedom from sin and fear.

See Thinking Further for Chapter 7 on page 141.

8. WORDS OF LIFE!

Who has ever seen anything like this? Who has ever had this problem before? There are too many people wanting to hear the Word of God!

The missionaries of Papua felt overwhelmed. Tribes had burned their power pieces in one valley after another, all over the land, dancing around the huge bonfires with great shouts and cheers and weeping. The charms and fetishes had weighed like heavy burdens on their backs, and now their hearts felt light. Would they gain eternal life immediately? Would their whole world change in a moment?

But all those ashes that were left behind by the piles of burning pig tails and net bags and broken spears and human skulls would grow nothing but weeds if the missionaries weren't quickly able to plant the seeds of truth.

"O, Lord, what can we do?" they prayed. "We haven't even fully learned their languages yet. How can we communicate Your gospel? Help, O Lord!"

Help came. Not only from Western missionaries, but from within Papua itself. New Christians like Jabonep came from among the tribal people, bringing the words of life that washed over those ash heaps of the soul and caused the garden of God to spring up in the hearts of people in one tribe after another.

"Listen! Listen!" The Dani tribes of the Toli Valley called to one another. "Real people are speaking the same words as the tuans!"

There beside the airstrip, next to the now-familiar airplane, stood the Toli Valley missionary Dave Martin, with some other people. Two of the new people were Dani men from the Ilaga Valley. But they were the sworn enemies of the Toli Valley Danis! The Toli Valley men picked up their spears and edged closer.

Their greased bodies trembled, their dark eyes opened wide in fear, but the Ilaga Valley men stood straight and tall.

"The words the tuans tell you are true!" cried the one called Jimbitu. He picked up a large stone. "Who made your spear?"

The men looked at their stone spearheads and said nothing. Of course they had made their spears themselves.

"Who made the wood and the stone for your spear?" continued Jimbitu. "You cannot make those things! Someone made them! It is the Great Maker."

The other missionary, Jagomi, spoke. "The Great Maker has worked in our stomachs. He has brought us His ki wone, His words of life!"

The Dani tribesmen stopped as if they had been turned into statues. Ki wone? Words of life?

Then one of the leaders stepped forward, snapping his fingers. "I am Tibala," he said. "We will hear more. Come." Jimbitu and Jagomi glanced at each other warily, but followed Tibala. The others went behind.

In the village, the men crouched together on the grass, in position for a serious talk. The women and children gazed in curiosity and fear to see their men talking with the enemy in such a way. What was happening?

Ki wone?

Hour after hour Jimbitu and Jagomi spoke, while Tibala and his tribe listened.

"You no longer have wars?" The Toli Valley Danis couldn't believe it. "You no longer fight and kill?" How could it be? Surely these were words of life!

"If we burn our power pieces, will we gain forever life?"

"No," said the witness men firmly. "Burning your power pieces will not gain you forever life. Neither will any of the other works and rules you talk about. Only Jesus Christ will give you forever life."

The men of the tribe couldn't sleep. At 3:00 in the morning they came to the hut where Jimbitu and Jagomi were sleeping. "Tell us some more of these ki wone," they said. "These are the words of life our ancestors have waited for." Through the night and into the day they asked questions and listened to the answers.

"We can't let the women find out," said one man. "They'll use this new knowledge against us."

"If the women hear our spirit talk, we'll have to kill them," said another.

"No," said Jagomi. "The Jesus way is for everyone. Women too. When they come to Him, they will no longer be witches. You won't need to kill them."

It was hard to believe, this new way.

"Is this nabelan kabelan?" asked one man. "Is it getting new skin like a snake instead of dying like the bird? Is this the forever life our ancestors lost?"

"Yes," said Jagomi. "Jesus Christ gives us nabelan kabelan. You were waiting for forever life. But you were also waiting for the Forever God. Jesus is the one you were waiting for."

Two of the pale missionaries who had come were Don and Eunice Richter, traveling the world with Gospel Recordings. For three days they worked at making recordings for the Toli Valley Danis.

"God is the greatest Spirit, who made everything," Eunice read from her paper.

Gordon Larson, who was with them, translated it into the Moni dialect.

Jimbitu listened, nodded, and translated it into the Ilaga Dani dialect.

One of the men from the Toli Valley listened and thought. Then he translated it into the Toli Valley dialect. These words he spoke into the little microphone Don had given him.

"God made man and woman. But the Enemy tempted them, and they sinned against God. They disobeyed God," Eunice read. Translation. Translation. Translation.

"But God promised that one day He would send a Rescuer. That Rescuer would crush the Enemy." The words flowed from one dialect to another.

Words of life.

Hour after hour, for three days, Eunice read one Bible story after another, and the other men translated.

Noah. Abraham. Moses. David. The prophets. John the Baptist. Jesus. Paul. When they were finished, there was the gospel, on a tape recorder, in the Toli Valley dialect.

When the three days were ended, life had changed in the Toli Valley. Hundreds of tribesmen accompanied Jimbitu and Jagomi back to the airstrip with the tuans.

Then Jimbitu turned to Tibala. "Why don't you take Jesus right now?" he asked.

Tibala looked surprised. "Am I ready?"

"You want His living words. You want to turn from the burden of your power pieces and the constant war. You know you have sin and need to be rescued. You are ready."

Tibala stood straight and tall. He raised his right arm to heaven. "Greetings, Lord!" he cried. "We have never met before, but I come to you now! Here in our valley we have heard Your living words for the first time. Make me strong in this new way, so that I can teach my people. That's it!"

The recordings traveled from village to village. All over the Toli Valley, men and women and children marveled at hearing their own talk out of the strange box. They listened to story after story, about the truth of God, the God who loves. They listened to the stories again and again.

They heard the words of life and turned to Jesus Christ.

See Thinking Further for Chapter 8 on page 141.

9. I SAW YOU IN MY DREAM

Dave and Esther Scovill both looked up in surprise. The door of their little grass-roofed house had burst open, and there stood a young Dani boy yelling and waving his hands and pointing outside.

Dave and Esther just gazed at him in wonder. They had arrived in this area of the Dani tribe only a few days before, and they didn't know the language. How could they possibly understand what this boy was trying to communicate? They peered out the door to try to see whatever he was pointing to as he continued to talk and gesture, but they saw nothing.

The boy's face showed his frustration, his shoulders sagged, and he heaved a sigh. He increased his volume, hoping that would help their understanding.

But Dave and Esther both simply shook their heads and lifted their hands with their palms upward. "We're sorry," they said. "We can't understand you."

Then the boy did something they understood. He smiled and pointed to the woodstove, making motions as if he were chopping wood.

"Do you want an axe?" Dave asked. The boy stood smiling.

"Well, let's get him one!" Esther cried. "Maybe he'll chop some wood for us!"

The boy took the axe and ran outside.

"What was that all about?" Dave asked.

"No way to tell now," his wife responded. "But Lord, help us to learn this language quickly. These people certainly do want to communicate!"

Before long, the boy returned, staggering under a load of firewood. Then he saw a bucket in the corner, grabbed it, and headed for the door again.

But before he walked out, he turned back to them. He spoke very slowly and clearly, as if he were talking to children. "Wat," he said, pointing to himself. Then he was gone.

"Wat," Dave repeated. "A gift from God."

Wat had come to work. But he had also come to teach. Even at twelve years old, he was an excellent language teacher. As he worked with Esther around the house, as he worked with Dave outside, he constantly taught.

More and more, they were able to communicate with each other.

As Dave and Esther learned new words and expressions, they began to teach Wat about the Great Sky Father who made all things, the sky, the clouds, the trees, the rocks, the rain.

Wat looked all around him, pondering this great spirit with so much power. "Is he bad?" he asked.

"No, very good," said Dave. "He loves people. He loves you."

Wat's eyes grew wide in disbelief. To think of a powerful spirit who *loves!*

One day, Wat taught Esther the word for "forever" and then asked, "Nonja, is the Great Spirit God a forever spirit?"

"Yes!" she said. "Yes, He is. And I will be forever with Him too."

Again Wat's eyes became large and round. "Nonja," he said, "will I be forever too?"

O Lord, how can I communicate? I have so few words in his language!

"You teach me more of your words," she answered, "and I will tell you."

As hard as Wat had worked before to teach the Scovills his language, he worked even harder now.

75

Hours and hours every day. It was almost as if he were the missionary, so desperately did he work.

Often during language training, Dave would open his Bible to try to tell Wat some of the great truths from it. Wat's cheerful face would become sober as he listened. Great Maker. Son who died. Men of badness. Live forever.

Live forever.

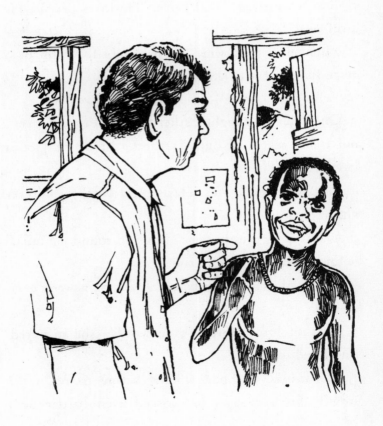

"We lost the way to live forever," said Wat one day. "The snake had it, because he could keep changing his skin, but the bird lost it. Our ancestors wanted to get the snake's skin, but instead they went the way of the bird."

Wat shook his head sadly. Then he looked up. "Tuan, I must speak a story to you. Does your mind hold the day you came to our people?"

"Yes, we remember it very well," said Dave. How could he forget? The western Danis had seen a few airplanes and pale people before. But every arrival— every airplane, every new pale person—was still an event to be celebrated. The day the Scovills had arrived, oh, what a party had greeted them! Hundreds of nearly naked dark-skinned people, some with bones in their noses just like the slides showed back at Prairie Bible Institute. Some with long necklaces and feathers and long, long matted hair held in net bags. Some with net bags full of sweet potatoes or even babies. All of them shouting, shouting, words the Scovills couldn't understand. Later they learned that the people were shouting, "Welcome my father! Welcome my mother!"

Wat's voice broke into Dave's reverie. "I was there."

But that was no surprise. Almost everyone was there. Dave nodded.

Wat spoke with more urgency. "I was there, in the crowd. And I saw you step off that whirra. You were holding that great Book. And I said, 'Oh! It's the man I saw in my dream!' "

Dave and Esther both looked at each other again, their eyebrows raised. "Your dream?"

"Yes! Some days before, I had a dream. I saw a man and his wife step out of a whirra. The man was holding a book. He was a big man. A very big man."

Dave smiled a little.

"My father and my mother, do you hold in your mind the day I came to your house?"

"Of course!" Esther said. "You were excited about something, but we couldn't understand you. Was it your dream?"

"Yes. I wanted to tell you that I saw you in my dream. And in my dream, I saw that I told you our words. And when you learned our words, you told me words from that Book.

"So when I saw you for the first time, I knew that you had come here to teach me. And I was ready to teach you, so you could tell those special words to us."

After only six weeks, Dave understood the Dani language well enough to tell a simple story. Wat helped him with the words he didn't know. In slow, stumbling language, with many mistakes, Dave spoke.

"Wat, Jesus told this story. A man planted good seeds in his garden. But while he was sleeping, his enemies came and planted weeds there. The good plants and the weeds grew together. The man knew that his enemy did it. But he said, 'I will wait until they are all grown. Then at harvest I'll gather the good food and I'll burn the weeds.'

"Later Jesus' followers came to him and asked him, 'What did that story mean?'

"Jesus said, 'I am the one who plants the true seed. The evil spirit called Satan plants the weeds. This garden is the whole world. The harvest is the end of the world. At the end of the world I will take all the wicked ones and burn them. I will take all the righteous ones to Myself, and they will shine like the sun.' "

Wat listened. "Those are good words, Tuan," he said. "These are the words you should speak at the meeting tomorrow."

"But I've been here only a short time," said Dave. "I can't speak well. I'll say wrong words."

"But this is a new story. We've heard the words from the black box many times. We know those stories," answered Wat. "Here. I'll tell you the words in good Dani." He handed Dave a piece of paper and a pen. "Put them on this banana leaf. You can speak these words tomorrow."

The next day, Dave looked out over the crowd of Danis who had come to listen to him. The mothers yelled at their children. The men laughingly called to each other. The old people began to fall asleep as soon as they sat down.

There must be nearly a thousand people here, Dave thought. *How can I possibly communicate? O, God, help me!*

With trembling hands, Dave stood and began to read the words he had carefully written out and practiced with Wat the day before. Slowly he pronounced the strange sounds.

Suddenly the men began to call for silence. Women put their hands over their children's mouths. Old people woke up.

They were listening. They were understanding.

Dave finished the story. He heaved a sigh and sat down. He was done.

But someone said, "Tuan Kobo. Those are good words. Tell them again."

With surprise, Dave stood up and read the words again. He saw the crowd all watching him with their full attention.

He finished reading. This time he stood and waited. The people waited too. Dave wasn't sure what to do.

Then an old woman said, "Tell us just once more."

This time, as Dave read slowly, he heard a low mumbling through the crowd. The people were memorizing his words!

At the end of the first sentence he stopped. The people held up one finger and mumbled the sentence he had said.

He read the second sentence. They all held up the second finger and repeated it.

On and on through the whole story. Through all their fingers. Through all their toes. Through their neighbors' fingers.

Then they rose to go.

"Tuan," said Wat. "I knew that was a good story. I knew the people would want to hear that one. Tonight they'll tell it around their fires. In the man hut, they won't talk about wars and spirits. They'll talk about that story."

Wat came to Christ and changed his name to another name that meant "with eyes only for heaven." He went on to become a teacher, pastor, and translator. Fifty years later he was an elder over a hundred churches in the Dani area.

See Thinking Further for Chapter 9 on page 141.

10. SPRINKLING COOL WATER

Don Richardson sat in the Sawi man hut, snapping his fingers to emphasize the importance of his words.

"This Jesus was the Son of the Greatest Spirit," he said. "He came as a man, doing great works to show His power."

Don kept talking, while one of the Sawi men repeated his words, sometimes changing them to help the other men understand. For a long time the men listened, some with interest, some with yawns.

Day after day Don talked with the men, telling them the most important story in the world. But Jesus was a Jew. What was a Jew? He wasn't a Sawi. He wasn't one of their ancestors. He lived long ago and far away. The Sawis became restless and uninterested.

Then one day Don told the story of Judas. "Remember, these were Jesus' close friends. For three years they walked with Him, talked with Him, ate with Him. But one man, Judas, planned to give Jesus over to the enemy."

Suddenly, no one was bored. Every hand stopped braiding vines or carving wood. Every eye was fastened on Don as he spoke. The men leaned forward to give their full attention.

Yes! thought Don. *The Word of God is capturing their hearts!*

"This man Judas," he continued, "sneaked out the very night that Jesus was eating a great feast with his own special friends. Judas went to the enemies and told them how they could capture Jesus, so they could kill Him. The enemies did capture Jesus that same night."

"Hoo!" the Sawi men listening caught their breaths. "Ha!" They all began to chatter with one another.

What are they saying? thought Don.

"Oh, Tuan!" cried one man. "That was doing with the caught pig!"

All the men together began to laugh. And laugh and laugh.

Don sat back in confusion. *What are they talking about?*

They laughed so hard they began to wipe their eyes with the tears from their laughter. They held their stomachs and rocked back and forth.

Why are they laughing? Obviously the Bible lesson was over for today. Don quietly climbed down the ladder, leaving the laughing men behind, snapping their fingers and thumping their chests.

Lord, what happened? What did I do? What did I say? He trudged slowly from the man hut back toward his own little house.

There was one of his language helpers. "Narai!" he called. "Can you help me?"

Narai came from the edge of the clearing. "I am here, Tuan," he said.

"Narai, I need you to explain something to me. What does this mean, something about doing something to a caught pig?"

"Oh, yes. " Narai nodded. "They were talking about it in the man hut, right? I can tell you. Tuan, you see the pigs around here?"

Don nodded. The pigs wandered here and there throughout the village and into the forest. They were always around.

"These are wild pigs, you know," said Narai.

"Well, not really wild," said Don. "You people capture them when they're small and feed them. And then they're half tame."

"Ah, yes, Tuan, but what will we do with them when they are full grown?"

"You'll eat them."

"That is what it means."

"What?" said Don. "I don't understand."

"We capture a pig and feed it, and it begins to trust us. Then, when it is time, we kill it. That is the same thing we do to a man."

"You mean, you get a man's trust, and then kill him?"

"Yes, Tuan. For Sawis, that's the best way to kill a man. That brings the most honor. Those are the stories we tell in our man hut year after year. Just a few years ago, we ate a man we had deceived so completely that he thought we were his dear friends." Narai began to smile at the memory. "That's one of our favorite stories."

Don's stomach felt sick, and his head hurt. The heat of the jungle began to weigh on him as it never had before. He didn't even swat at the mosquito that buzzed around his sweating face.

Is this where we are, Lord? In a place where Judas is the hero instead of Jesus?

He wanted to lie down. He wanted to get away. He wanted to go far away.

There was Carol in their little house, applying iodine to another man's spear wound. They had been living here among the villages of the Sawi tribe for only a few months. It seemed that almost every day someone was coming for help with a wound from a fight or a battle.

Every day the Richardsons talked to the Sawis about how terrible it was to keep fighting and killing, to keep hurting each other. But the Sawi always said, "Oh, you tuans just don't understand."

That night Don tossed in his sleep. He dreamed about other missionaries who had said, "It's too hard to work with the adults. They don't want to listen. They're too attached to their old ways. They aren't interested in Jesus. We're just going to start schools for the children, and give them the gospel. We can't work with the adults." He woke up and lay gazing into the darkness. *Lord, isn't Your Truth strong enough to win the hearts of these people? I don't want to leave them in darkness and just work with the children! I want to win the men!*

Don kept going to the man hut. He told the Sawis the story of the death of Jesus, the death of Judas, and the glorious resurrection. But the Sawi were disappointed. They wanted that deceiver Judas to be the hero of the story.

"O God!" Don cried out. "What can I do? How can I help a culture that's so twisted that it honors cruel deceivers and despises Your own Son? What can I do?"

Day after day Don and Carol cried out to God together. Every day they gave the Sawis the medicine to heal their bodies, asking God how in the world they could give them the medicine that would heal their spirits.

"Tuan, my back!" A woman came running to the house, her back torn and bleeding.

"What happened?" Carol gasped.

"My husband was angry," the woman answered simply, sinking down onto the floor.

Suddenly, a dozen men appeared in the clearing, painted with colored ashes, with bright feathers, waving their spears and shrieking.

"Not again," Carol moaned.

Don closed the door and watched out the crack. "I've lost count of how many battles they've waged

here. These two villages … Carol, we're trying to bring them together to hear the gospel, but the more they come together, the more they fight each other."

"Well, it's no wonder," said Carol, tenderly applying a cool cloth to the woman's back. "They don't value life. They love violence. They love lying and deceit." She began to choke back a sob as the woman on the floor moaned. "What can we do?"

Ask God what to do. Keep seeking God. Don't give up. The thought came to both of them.

So Don and Carol continued to pray, and to ask others to pray.

One day Don read Ephesians 6:19. Paul had asked his Ephesian friends to pray for him, "that utterance may be given unto me, that I may open my mouth boldly, to make known the mystery of the gospel."

"I want to make known that mystery, O Lord!" Don prayed. "I want to open my mouth boldly. But O Lord, You must make a way for my words to be received!"

Ephesians 6. The chapter that describes spiritual warfare. O Lord, this is spiritual warfare that we're fighting. We want Your shield of faith. Your breastplate of righteousness. We want our feet to be covered with the gospel of peace. In Sawi the expression for peace was "cool water." *The gospel of cool water—how I would love for them to receive that. But how?*

Day after day, as the wars continued to rage before their eyes, Don and Carol and their small son Stephen saw men from the different villages fighting each other. Sometimes it was even people in the very same village, angry over a stolen pig or a sarcastic word. Fighting, wounding. More and more. Week after week Carol tended to the wounds. Don yelled at the men to stop their fighting, but they would simply look at him and say, "Tuan, you don't understand."

This has been going on for centuries, spoke a voice in Don's ear. *What makes you think you can bring it to an end?*

"Carol," Don finally said, "If we move away, maybe go to another village far away, then these two villages can separate again and they won't keep fighting each other."

"Yes, they will," said Carol. "They've been doing it for generations."

"I know, but maybe it wouldn't happen as much. They could each go back into the jungle and stay away from each other. I've been trying to bring them together, but until Jesus Christ changes their hearts, what can we do?"

Together Don and Carol prayed. Maybe leaving really was what God wanted them to do.

That night, Don went to the man hut in one of the villages. "My family and I will go," he said. "You're warring more and more, and you can't listen to our words. We'll find a different village somewhere."

Then he went to the man hut of the second village and said the same words. "We're going."

All fighting ceased as the men of each village gathered in their own man hut to discuss this important announcement. The tuan was leaving. What would they do?

"Well, if we're going, who knows what they might do to us?" said Carol. "We won't be here to give them the shells and axes anymore."

"I'd already thought of that," said Don. "But we're in the Lord's hands."

That night, a call came from outside the door. "Tuan!"

Don took a flashlight to see the faces of several of the men from the village. "Don't leave us!" they said.

"But you'll kill each other if I stay," Don answered.

"No, Tuan," said one man. "Tomorrow we'll sprinkle cool water on each other."

"Cool water?" said Don. "You'll make peace?"

See Thinking Further for Chapter 10 on page 142.

11. PEACE CHILD

Don and Carol lay in bed whispering to each other. "How can they possibly make peace? Everyone lies, everyone deceives. They can be as friendly as you please to their enemies, but that might be the beginning of fattening them like a pig for the slaughter. They honor people like Judas. Nobody trusts anybody!"

They slept little that night.

The next morning when they arose and peered out their window, they saw nothing unusual. Except . . . the unusual thing was that they didn't see any people at all.

But then one man began to climb down his ladder with a child. His wife followed, weeping. Suddenly people began to stream out of their houses.

The man headed toward the other village. But the mother grabbed the baby, screaming, and ran back to her house, where her relatives protected her.

What was happening?

A man from the neighboring village appeared, again holding a baby. Again the baby's mother grabbed the baby and ran.

What kind of drama were they playing out?

Knots of people milled about the village, tense, expectant, some of them moaning. Don and Carol and Stephen stood on their little porch, watching, wondering.

Suddenly, one man from the neighboring village broke through the crowd. He too was holding a baby.

In the distance sounded a scream, but it was too late. The man held out his baby to one of the men of this village. "I will give my child to you," he said. "You will take my name."

Another man ran into his own hut and returned. "I will give my child," he said. "And you will take my name."

Don and Carol watched the nervous crowd, some shouting, some wailing. They listened to the mothers of the two little boys, screaming in agony.

"My son! My son!"

What would happen to the little boys?

"Eehaa!" cried one of the men. "We will sprinkle cool water on both of our villages!"

The men took the little boys and began to decorate them with armbands of vines and palm fibers. Young people in both villages began to beat the drums and dance. Except for the wailing mothers, all of the people had turned from mourning to dancing.

"Ari!" Don called one of the young men aside. "What was all this? What happened?"

Ari looked at Don in disbelief. "Tuan, haven't you ever seen a peace child before? Maybe tuans never fight with each other, so they never need to make peace."

"No, I don't know about it. This is not part of my culture," Don answered. "What will happen to the babies?" His stomach knotted in fear.

"Oh, we'll care for this baby, Tuan. And the other village will care for ours. As long as the peace child lives, there will be peace between our villages. That's why we celebrate now!"

People from the two villages approached each other and exchanged gifts—necklaces, knives, shells. They exchanged names, too, as each man took a name from someone in the other village. Then, around a big bonfire, the two groups of former enemies danced with each other. One group around the other. Then the other group around the first. Laughing and shouting.

Cool water. Peace.

"It's the only way, Tuan," Ari explained. "Any other promises we won't believe. But with the peace child, we know the promise of cool water is true."

A man held one of the babies high. "We will protect him!" he cried. "We will sprinkle cool water!"

The other man did the same. And the crowd cheered and cheered and cheered.

Before long, Don was able once again to climb the vine ladder to the man hut. "I have new words for you," he said, snapping his fingers.

The men gazed at him, wondering what the words would be this time.

"You know that when you gave the peace child, I cried out. I wished there could be another way to make peace."

The men murmured their agreement. If only there could be another way!

"But I know that you're right," Don continued. "There is no other way. And that's why . . ." He paused to be sure he had the attention of every man in the man house. "That's why the Greatest Spirit gave a peace child too."

All eyes were on him. The Greatest Spirit gave a peace child?

"When a man gives a peace child, he gives his very own son, yes?"

"Yes," replied the men.

"And you have cool water as long as the peace child lives, yes?"

"Yes," said the men.

"The Greatest Spirit needed to sprinkle cool water between Himself and all the world. Who would be a peace child great enough for this? Who would be a peace child who would live long enough for this?" Don snapped his fingers and thumped the gourd that lay beside him.

"That Jesus you told us about, He was the peace child?" one of the men asked.

"Yes!" cried Don. "He was the peace child for the whole world!"

"So when that man Judas betrayed Him, he was killing a peace child." All the room erupted in angry tones. There was nothing worse than killing a peace child. That would mean war that would never end!

"But Jesus rose again from the dead," Don reminded them. "And He lives forever. He is the eternal peace child. " He held up his Bible. "These holy leaves tell me that He is the Prince of Peace." Then he read to them, in the Sawi language, John 3:16.

"You took that baby into your home to be the peace child from the other village. But Jesus is the Peace Child of God. You cannot take Him into your home in the same way. You can receive Him into your spirit. He will live in you and give you His Name.

"Remember," said Don. "The cool water you gain through your peace child will end, because the child will die someday. This peace is weak. But the peace that God gives is strong! Jesus Christ will bring the cool springs of clear water!"

The men knew that what Don said was true. Their peace was weak.

More days passed. The men talked and asked questions and watched Don and Carol in all that they did. They saw the Richardsons trust God in deep trial. They could tell these tuans had the cool water from the Greatest Spirit.

Then came the time when one after another stood in the man hut and proclaimed, "I want to receive the Peace Child from God. I'm ready to trust in Jesus."

Over the course of two years, hundreds came to Christ and began to learn to read from His holy leaves.

From fear to hope. From turmoil to peace. Cool water flowed down from heaven on the people of the Sawi tribe.

See Thinking Further for Chapter 11 on page 142.

12. CHANGES IN CHURCH

Throughout the Toli Valley, the Danis were preparing for the Sunday meeting. The men worked their pig-grease-coated fingers through their long hair to form ringlets down their backs, and then adorned it with their best and brightest feathers. They slathered fresh pig grease mixed with soot all over their bodies.

Hours before the meeting time, the men began to gather, circling around and brandishing their ten-foot spears as if they were preparing for battle. They tossed their heavy curls from side to side, showing off for the women, who peeked out from behind the doors.

They ran and danced, yelled and sang, until the sweat ran from their glistening bodies. They chanted the only songs they knew, songs about killing their enemies and cutting their bodies apart.

Finally, the time came. The men, with the women following quietly behind, arrived at the field beside the airstrip and laid their spears in neat piles. Then they sat down to listen to John Dekker teach them.

John Dekker stood and held up his open Bible. "I want to tell you a story that Jesus told. He said that a man cleaned his house. He got out the bad spirit that had been in his house. But then his house stood empty. Because his house was empty, seven spirits that were even worse came into the house.

"You Danis are like a house that you have cleaned. You cleaned the house and threw out the spirits by burning your power pieces. But the Words of Life tell us that if you leave the house empty, seven times as many evil spirits will enter. Your house cannot be filled with your new talk or your good works. Your house must be filled with Jesus Christ.

"Some of you want to come only to follow your group. But some of you really do want to learn the Jesus way. So tomorrow morning, we'll teach more of God's words. Our teaching will start when the sun is between those two mountains, so you'll need to come very early."

John felt sure that if the meeting were held early enough, most of the people wouldn't come. So he was surprised when he heard voices the next morning while it was still completely dark.

He went outside. "What are you doing out here? It's still night!"

"But Tuan," the people said. "You said to come early."

More and more came. By 8:00 over a thousand people had gathered.

John knew he couldn't really teach such large groups the way he wanted to be able to teach them. He decided to do what other missionaries in other parts of the land had done: he asked some of the village leaders to choose about twenty men who were leaders themselves and who wanted to learn more about eternal life in Jesus Christ. Then the men came with their wives, and the witness schools began in John's part of the Toli Valley. Four times a week they gathered, and John taught them a Bible lesson and a Bible verse.

One day, one of the men in John's school asked, "What was the name of that father of the pale people, the one made out of dirt?"

"His name was Adam," John replied.

"And what was the name of the father of the real people—I mean the dark people?"

"That was the same man. Adam. He was the ancestor of all people, dark and light, big and small."

"This is true, Tuan? We have the same ancestor?"

"It's true. We read it in the words of God."

"But Tuan, we know that dark men walked away from God. Pale men have always walked with God. That's why you know God's words."

"No. *All* men walked away from God. God gave His own Son to bring us back to Himself. All of us need to be brought to Jesus, to walk the Jesus path." John held up his Bible. "There was a time when I didn't know God. I had to come to Him through Jesus Christ too, just like you. Every man in all the world needs God's words so that we can come to the Living Word, Jesus Christ."

Almost every day the witness men memorized a new story and a new verse, and then they went out to all parts of the valley to teach the people in the distant villages. Wherever they went, people from the whole area came together to listen to their good words. The long-lost secret of eternal life was being revealed.

Not only in the Toli Valley, but all through the land, witness men who had been taught in the witness schools took the Words of Life to tell people about the Living Word, Jesus Christ.

"How can we teach the people who won't come to our meetings?" some of the witness men pondered.

One said, "I have a large piece of ground that needs to be cleared. When people come to help me, I'll give a feast. Usually when we eat a feast, we talk about war plans or stolen pigs. But this time we'll preach to them."

Some tribal leaders muttered curses against the new Christians gathering at the witness schools. "Don't go to listen to those tuans! They want to destroy our way of life. Our way of life is about war. You can't leave it."

But the new Christians answered bravely. "Our old way of life is full of sin and killing and fear. The living words are words of hope and love and peace. This Spirit is a good Spirit. We must listen."

A few new Christians had to do something no one in their village had ever done. Because their clans threatened to kill them, they had to leave the group. They gathered with others and started a new village. "Don't fear," one witness man told them. "If our people kill us, we will go to be with Jesus."

One day before Sunday meeting began, a handsome man named Rigwi sat fingering his long black braided hair.

"Your hair looks very nice," said the missionary.

Rigwi's face contorted in anger. "Why do you speak good words about my hair?" he sneered. "Don't you know I grow my hair like this to shake it at the women and at the spirits? Why do you talk about it looking nice?"

Suddenly Rigwi stood. "This hair is of the old way. I will be rid of it." He turned to the other Christians who had gathered. "You may want to keep your hair, but not me." Then to everyone's surprise he stomped away.

When Rigwi returned, his hair was gone. "This is good." He smiled. "That was part of the old way. I am done with the old way. I want to follow the Jesus path."

As more and more men chose to cut their hair to cut off the connection with the spirits and the proud displays of their manliness, they also began to stop the wild dancing and war songs before the church meeting. More and more they began to form new songs of their own to show their love for their Savior.

We love Jesus very much.
He died for us.
Jesus took the sweet potato and thanked God.
Jesus' body was broken for us, like the sweet potatoes are broken.
His body was broken for you.
His body was broken for me.
We love Jesus very much.

Jesus took the juice and thanked God.

His blood flowed down for me.

His blood paid for you.

His blood washed my sins.

His blood took away your sins.

Jesus died for us.

We are gathered together here.

We are thinking about the death of Christ.

We are thinking that Christ will come.

We will go to heaven to be with Him.

We love Jesus very much.

He died for us.

See Thinking Further for

Chapter 12 on page 142.

13. THE SPIRIT WHO LOVES

Spirits have come! Spirits have come!
The message ran through the village like a shock wave, and to the villages beyond. "They look like real men, but they are faded like ghosts!"

It was 1963, several years since the first Western missionaries had come to Papua, but the Kimyal tribe had heard nothing about that. They knew of no people in the world but themselves.

The two exhausted men, Phil Masters and Bruno DeLeeuw, stood in the clearing, holding their hands out and open to show that they meant no harm. How could they even begin to describe the distance they had traveled in order to cut through razor grass with machetes to reach this tribe? The days and days of trekking through mud and over rocks and through rivers? "We come in peace," they said in the Dani language, hoping that someone might understand.

But the Kimyal tribesmen did not respond. They stood silent, surrounding the men with spears lifted, ready to strike.

"What should we do?" one asked the leader.

"They are powerful spirits," muttered the chief. "We must capture them and keep them in the spirit hut. Then the witch doctor will tell us if we should kill them."

Phil reached into his backpack as all the black eyes followed his every move. He whispered something quietly to Bruno, who did the same. "Here." He held out his hand, speaking aloud in Dani, even though it seemed that no one could understand him. "This is a peace offering. See?" His hand cupped something that looked like a white powder, and he lifted it to his tongue. He tasted it, closed his eyes, and smiled. "Mmmm."

The Kimyals, in spite of their fear, drew closer.

"What is it? Who will taste it?" Some men pulled back. Some inched forward. But no one reached out.

Then the witch doctor's son stepped up. "I will taste it," he said. He reached out to the hand of the ghostly man. Between his fingers he took a bit of the white powder and touched it to the tip of his tongue. The biting taste made his eyes light up with delight. "Ah!" he cried out. He reached for more.

Suddenly, the warriors lowered their spears and surged forward. "No, Siud! You can't have it all! Let us have some!" One dark hand after another reached to pinch some of the white stuff that Phil and Bruno held out. One set of eyes after another lit with pleasure.

"Well, Phil," Bruno asked under the chorus of exclamations. "Do you think God is using this salt to save our lives?"

Salt opened the door for Phil and Bruno, allowing them to settle in the Kimyal village. They followed the path other missionaries before them had followed:

buying some land with a steel axe, hiring workers to help them build a house and clear land for an airstrip.

The boy Siud, who first tasted the salt, seemed especially interested in the spirit-men. He watched Phil's kindness and gentleness and hard work. He helped him learn the language. When Phil's wife Phyliss and their children joined him, Siud spent time with the family.

Some days Phil would count on his fingers to seven and say, "Today, no work. Stories." Then he walked from village to village to speak about the greatest Spirit, the Spirit of the Sky, who wanted people to be able to call Him Father. The Spirit of love, the Sky Father and His Son Jesus Christ, who brought salvation from sin.

Every Sunday, Siud followed, listening, helping. One day, after months had passed, Siud said, "Tuan, did you know I was waiting for you?"

"What do you mean?" asked Phil.

"Many suns before you came to our village, when I was just a child, I stood out on that ridge." Siud pointed to a peak at the edge of the river gorge. "I decided I would not study to be a witch doctor like my father. I hated and feared the spirits. I hated the ways of our people.

"All the spirits in our land are spirits of hate and fear. But deep in here, in my stomach, I thought that there must be a Spirit who loves. I never told my people my thoughts, because I knew they would think I was crazy, and they would throw me into the river." Siud gazed out into the sky. "But I thought, someday I will learn about the Spirit who loves, and I will know Him, and I will love Him.

"Then you came, and you were kind. I thought you might be the Spirit who loves, but you told me that you are just a man like us. But you brought a message from the true Spirit.

"So, I was waiting for you. I was ready to hear your good words about the great Sky Father who is over all the other spirits."

"In our land, we say that Sky Father made your heart ready," Phil answered. "Or your stomach."

Siud touched Phil's clothing. "You wear coverings like spider webs," he said. "We have an old legend that someday a spirit being would come from another world wearing spider webs, bringing us an important message."

"It's the most important message of all," said Phil, gazing at the towering mountains. "A message that will bring peace into this world."

Siud sighed. "That's good," he said. "Because the world is full of hate and fear and killing. We need words of peace. We need the Spirit who loves.

"Tuan," Siud added, "I listen to you talk to the Spirit who loves, and I want to learn to talk to Him too. I want to know those good words that you know."

"We'll teach you more," said Phil. "We'll be glad to teach you to pray. The Sky Father will give you strength and power against the evil spirits. We'll teach you the Bible. We'll even teach you to read these good words."

That night Siud lay in the man hut awake for hours, talking to the Spirit who loves. He felt his whole body alive with joy. To think that the same Spirit with more power than any of them had imagined would also be the Spirit with such love that Siud couldn't even comprehend it! And this spirit of the Sky wanted His people to talk with Him and call Him "Father."

Less than five years later, after teaching Siud and other young men week in and week out, Phil Masters and another missionary became martyrs for the cause of Christ. They were killed by a neighboring tribe.

For weeks Siud mourned. But Phil had left behind cassette tapes and wind-up cassette players. Again Siud could listen to Phil's voice telling the familiar stories. He traveled from village to village playing the recordings for his people to hear. Never did he tire of these stories. He loved the Savior who loved him.

Then other missionaries came. Some for a short time, others for years. Elinor Young was one who came to begin the long work of translating the New Testament. Orin and Rosa Kidd came to teach.

When Orin and Rosa had been in Korupun for a while, Siud confessed, "We know Jesus Christ, but we are like babies. We're so glad you have come to teach us more."

Orin taught as Elinor interpreted. He especially wanted to teach the men to learn the Bible for themselves.

"Listen, Siud," he said one day. "Elinor just translated this. It's from the last book of the Bible, the book of Revelation."

Siud listened as Orin read in the Kimyal language, "I looked, and there before me was a great multitude that no one could count, from every nation, tribe, people, and language, standing before the throne, in front of the Lamb. They wore white robes and held branches in their hands. And they cried out in a loud voice: 'Salvation belongs to our God, who sits on the throne, and to the Lamb.'"

Siud closed his eyes, listening to the electrifying words for the first time. "This means," he said, "this means that people from all nations will praise Jesus Christ together?"

"Yes, all. Together."

"The Kimyals too?"

"The Kimyals too."

"We will all stand before the great throne of the great God together." Siud kept repeating it. "The Kimyals too."

The young pastors knew the Bible stories well. They could tell the story of Jesus' birth to their people. But when they began to learn to read the Bible for themselves, they didn't understand some parts.

"Tuan Kidd, what does this mean?" one of the young men asked. "We don't understand it."

"What is it?" Orin asked. "Read it to me."

The young man read Romans 6:4. *"We are buried with Him by baptism into death, so that just as the glory of God the Father raised up Christ from the dead, in that same way we also can walk in newness of life."*

"What does it mean?" asked the young man.

"I've talked to you about baptism, and how it's a picture of your new life," said Orin. "Now, you figure out what this means. You ask the Holy Spirit to open the eyes of your understanding."

All of the young men were silent, reading the Scripture and praying.

Then suddenly, Siud jumped up. He was almost trembling. "Tuan, the Lord spoke to me! I understand it! It means that we were *in Christ* when He died! We were *in Christ* when He rose again! It means that Jesus has broken the power of sin in our lives! We can live holy lives in the power of the Holy Spirit!

"Tuan Kidd!" Siud exclaimed. "I will teach my people this Sunday!"

See Thinking Further for Chapter 13 on page 142.

14. BAD LEGS WOMAN

Siud, the pastor, stood and held up his hands for silence. All around him, the jolly Kimyal people stopped their laughing, stopped their eating, to listen.

"We are having this feast to welcome back our friend and mother." He pointed to Elinor Young, the Bible translator, who had just arrived back in their village after being in the U.S. for several months. "Now," he announced, "her name will be Bad Legs Woman."

"Bad Legs! Bad Legs Woman! Welcome back!" The people of the Kimyal tribe seemed to be very pleased to welcome Elinor with those words.

"Hello, Bad Legs Woman!" one of the Kimyals called. "We're glad you came back to us. You were gone too long. I want to work with you on the translation again."

Elinor knew the Kimyal people loved her. She had lived among them, here in the midst of these towering mountains and deep gorges, for sixteen years, learning their language, telling them about the great God and

His Son Jesus Christ, beginning the long work of translating the Bible. The Kimyals, small and lively, loved the fact that she was no taller than they were. And it was obvious she had bad legs! *But I know there's got to be another reason for this name,* she mused.

Elinor's mind flipped through the pages of her childhood and youth.

"The polio has paralyzed her," the doctors told the child's parents. "Even if she lives, she'll probably never get out of bed again." But Elinor's parents worked and worked and worked to help their little girl walk. Her brothers and sister, her friends at school, everyone helped.

Elinor grew in strength and began to walk with crutches and braces. By the time she was about nine, she began to feel that God wanted her to be a missionary one day. When she was thirteen, she thought, *I know that's what God wants me to do.*

"You, a missionary?" Even if people didn't actually say the words, their faces showed their disbelief. "You can hardly even walk!"

But Elinor became stronger and attended Prairie Bible Institute, with every intention of taking the gospel some place far away, even if she needed to use those crutches.

Now, as she carefully moved her tiny body around, listening to the happy greetings from the Kimyals, her mind returned to her first year here at the village of Korupun. Sitting at the edge of the little airstrip, gazing down into the deep river gorge where the white waters roared and tumbled, working to learn the language, she had told the story of her bad legs. "The doctor said to my parents that I might die."

"But you didn't," one of the boys had replied, "because God wanted you here to bring us His Good News in our own language."

Now he was a man, fifteen years older, greeting her. "Hello, Bad Legs Woman!" His face was alight with smiles.

One day, the missionary finally had a chance to ask Pastor Siud about her strange name. "Siud, why are people calling me Bad Legs Woman?"

Pastor Siud stood only a little taller than Elinor herself. "Didn't you listen to what I said at our feast? I announced to everyone that this is your name now."

"Oh, uh, well, I guess I didn't hear that. But I was wondering what it really means. Why are my bad legs so important?"

Siud looked at her in surprise. "Bad Legs Woman, don't you see? Look at our people."

Elinor looked around. She watched them chopping at their sweet potato gardens and tending their pigs.

"If any of our people have bad legs," Siud said, "you know that they will never go anywhere. They can't even leave this valley. But you, even with your bad legs, you have come all the way from your other world to tell us about Jesus Christ."

A long, long way. Siud still didn't know how far, but he was beginning to learn just how big the world truly was. Just how far Elinor had really come.

"Bad Legs, you know that different pale people have brought God's Word to our tribe. Most of them are a lot taller than we are. Some of them are much stronger too, and they all have good legs. For one reason or another almost all of them have left us. But even though you are small and weak, you have stayed and stayed. You have worked with our people to translate the Word of God. God gave you to us with your bad legs, because He loves us and He wants us to learn His Word. Your bad legs are a gift to us from God."

One day, a Kimyal elder came to Elinor's office and said, "Bad Legs, there will be a baptism and feast in Duram. We're all going." Before the Kimyals had come to Christ, they killed quickly and easily. They called down curses on their enemies. Before, Duram was enemy territory. But now all that was changed. Instead of making war, the Kimyal clans made trails and bridges.

"All our people are coming," the elder repeated. "We want you to come too. We'll take you in your mountain carrier." Elinor called it her MTS, her Mountain Transport System. Her net-and-board carrier sat between two strong poles that the Kimyal men could carry, so that she could get anywhere she needed to go.

The next morning, six small men appeared at Elinor's door to carry her the two-hour trek to Duram for the baptism and feast. Four carried her in her MTS, and two ran along beside, ready to take a turn when the others grew tired.

Off they went like mountain goats, over impossible trails. Skinny paths only a few inches wide, along the sides of sheer mountain cliffs with torrential rivers below. "The path is straight and good," they promised. Elinor chuckled, because she knew better. She gazed from her MTS at the roaring, laughing waterfalls leaping down the faces of the cliffs. "I love you, Korupun," she whispered. "You're the most beautiful place on earth. These are the most beautiful people on earth."

As the path led down and down, Elinor gazed up and up, at the green and lofty peaks. "I lift my eyes to the hills," she murmured. "Thank you, God, for bringing me here. Thank you for the Kimyals." She watched a landslide on a distant mountain, reminding her of the power greater than those strong hills.

The carriers approached the raging river, where a long narrow bridge made of poles and vines hung suspended from one cliff to the other, thirty feet above the river. It was wide enough for only one person at a time, walking carefully with one foot in front of the other.

How many times had Elinor crossed this delicate bridge in her MTS? Countless times. She rather enjoyed the feeling of the bridge swinging from side to side under her as her carriers ran.

But this day, even before the carriers stepped on, she saw that the bridge seemed almost broken—it was hanging in a strange way. Two men took the poles; the

other four fell in line single file behind them. As her carriers stepped on and began to take one careful step after another, Elinor looked down at the huge boulders in the foaming river. *Well, if the vines snap, we won't be in pain for long. You know that our lives are always in Your hands, Lord.*

The men inched along the dangerous bridge, one small step at a time. Elinor closed her eyes and smiled. *You'll bear them up in Your hands, Lord. We're in Your hands.*

And then, they were on the other side. "We won't go that way on the way back, Bad Legs Woman!" one of them said. "On the way back, we'll cross on the rocks." Elinor looked down at the foaming water splashing in torrents over the rocks. Not much comfort in that thought. *Either way I'll trust You, Lord*, thought Elinor. *As long as You have work for me here, You'll keep me safe.*

When they arrived in Duram, Elinor's carriers set her down outside the village where the pigs were roasting and the baptism would be held.

"Welcome, Bad Legs Woman!" the people of Duram cried. They hugged her. "We're so glad to see you."

The people kept coming until over a hundred had gathered for this baptism. Down the hill they climbed to the river where the Kimyals had built a small dam. Just for a while, they forced some of the water to turn aside into a muddy pool.

Three Kimyal pastors preached the Word of God to the crowd. Then they climbed down into the pond, with two men, an old woman, and two teenagers.

"My heart is no longer heavy," said one man. "Now my great burden is gone!"

"I no longer need to sacrifice pigs!" cried the other man. "Now Jesus Christ is my only sacrifice!"

One teenager said, "I used to live in darkness, but now I walk in the path of light!"

The other teenager said. "I have confessed all my sins, and they are washed clean by the blood of Jesus Christ!"

The old woman cried out, "I will teach this great Way to my children and my children's children!"

Then one of the pastors called out, "In Sky Father's Name, in Jesus Christ's Name, in Holy Spirit's Name, we baptize you!" The pastors baptized one, and another, and another.

The singing and the praising went on and on. God had brought them His great salvation through Jesus Christ. Peace filled their hearts and their valleys. And Elinor, Bad Legs Woman, filled with joy, praised God together with them.

See Thinking Further for Chapter 14 on page 143.

15. BIBLE PARTY

Siud, the Kimyal elder, sighed as he sat with the missionaries. "If only we could have the Scriptures in our own language. Pray that God will do that for us."

When the first missionaries had come years before, they found that the Kimyals, like every other Papuan tribe, had no written language. Phil Masters began to try to make an alphabet for them, but then he was killed. Elinor Young, Bad Legs Woman, had translated part of the New Testament, but then sickness had forced her to return to the United States.

Now years had gone by. And still the Kimyals didn't have the Bible in their own language.

Night after night when Orin and Rosa Kidd asked how they could pray, Siud and the other elders answered the same. "We need to be able to read the Scriptures in our own words. That's the way for us to really understand them."

"Yes," said Rosa. "We want to keep praying about that."

More and more, as the Kimyal Christians prayed, Orin and Rosa heard this heavy sigh of the soul.

"O God!" Siud prayed. "You promised Simeon that he would not die before he saw Jesus Christ! O God! You are promising me that I will not die until I see the Scriptures in my hands to teach my people, Your people, O God, the Kimyals!"

Orin and Rosa listened to the prayers. Orin's time was full with his teaching and training. *Maybe God wants me to do this,* thought Rosa. *But I have no training and feel so inadequate for this task. I'm afraid of making mistakes and giving the Kimyal people something less than God's holy Word. Is He really asking me to do this?*

"Rosa," God's voice kept saying to her. "This isn't about you. This is about Me."

For two months she wrestled. As time passed, she became more and more sure that God wanted her to take on the translation work. One day when she was reading in Exodus, Rosa saw a verse that seemed to be for her. "God said, I will be with you. And this will be a sign to you that it is I who have sent you: when you have brought the people out of Egypt, you will worship God on this mountain."

Rosa looked out her little window, where the great mountains towered around her. Already the valley where she sat was higher than the Appalachian Mountains in the U.S. "Yes, Lord," said Rosa. "With Your help, I'll do it. You'll be with me, and I surrender to You my mind, my hands, and my body to do Your will. Use me for Your glory. I believe Your promise to me that we will worship You on this mountain."

Five years passed. Ten years. Twelve years. Rosa and her faithful Kimyal helpers continued to work on the Kimyal translation of the New Testament. A long, long time.

Finally ...

"The Bibles are ready to be printed! The New Testaments are coming!" Word spread through village after village of the Kimyal tribe. It was early in 2010, and they had been waiting for the complete New Testaments in their languages since they had first begun to receive the gospel, over forty years earlier.

Celebrations began weeks before the New Testaments actually arrived, as the people stayed up late singing their praises to God for bringing His Word to them in their own language.

Plane after plane landed on the tiny gravel strip 6000 feet high, bringing in people for the dedication. Missionaries came who hadn't been there in years, including Phyliss Masters, whose husband Phil had been killed. And Elinor Young, Bad Legs Woman, who had translated a third of the New Testament before she had to leave. Every missionary was greeted with singing, hugging, dancing, and praising.

The Kimyal people, their faces alight with the joy of Jesus Christ, began to kill pigs for the feast. Dozens, hundreds of pigs were slaughtered. "All those years you gave your lives to us!" Pastor Siud told the missionaries. "Now we want to give to you."

Then came the airplane with the New Testaments. People were so excited that they began to cry and sing

and yell. *God's Word was finally coming to them in their own language!*

Pastor Siud received the box. Then he called the people to silence and began to pray.

"O God! O God! The plan that You had from the beginning regarding Your Kimyals, which already existed in your Spirit, the month that you had set, the day that you had set, has come to pass today!

"O my Father, my Father! You looked at all the different languages and chose which ones would be put into Your Word. You decided that we should see Your Word in our own language.

"O God, today You have placed Your Word into my hands, just as You promised. You have placed it here in our land.

"And for all this, O God, I give you praise!"

The valley erupted with cheers and singing, weeping and praising. The New Testament had come. The people had the Word of God in their own language. They had been brought out of the land of darkness. And they worshipped God together on that mountain.

See Thinking Further for Chapter 15 on page 143.

A MESSAGE FROM THE AUTHOR

In February of 2011, my husband Tim, during family devotions, said, "I want to show you something." He led us to the computer and showed us a video that was being passed around Facebook. It was a video of a tribe of people, some wearing Western clothes, but others dressed in their most beautiful celebration garb with huge feather headdresses, many of them carrying spears, as if in a parade. All of them were singing, dancing, shouting, in eager anticipation of the arrival of an airplane.

"What's happening?" I asked. *And why were we watching this video during family devotion time?*

"Just wait and see," said my husband.

The tiny airplane arrived, touching down on a strip barely wide enough and long enough for it to land between the towering mountain and the river gorge.

The boxes began to be unloaded, full of New Testaments. The tribal people began to weep.

Then an older man filled with the Holy Spirit— the words on the screen said his name was Siud—cried out his thanksgiving to God for finally giving the New Testament to the Kimyals.

The video, put out by World Team, brought me to tears, but I was filled with questions. "Who are these people? Why such powerful emotions? So many Christians!"

This experience led me on a treasure hunt that involved months of research, reading old newspaper articles and missionary bulletins, ordering books online and renewing library books again and again, and best of all, communicating with several gracious missionaries who had worked here and there among the dozens and dozens of tribes in the highlands of Papua, Indonesia.

And now, when I watch that same video again, I feel that I am there. These are my brothers and sisters. One day, I'll meet them, and together we'll praise the God of heaven, we'll praise our Savior Jesus Christ, who—astoundingly, incredibly—has loved us and delivered us from fear and given us His Holy Word.

ABOUT THE MISSIONARIES

Chapter 2 "Across the World": Ebenezer Vine, the head of Regions Beyond Missionary Union (now called World Team) was a man of vision who often presented his vision to the students of various Bible and missionary colleges. His story is told more fully in *Drumbeats that Changed the World*, by Joseph F. Conley.

Chapter 3 "The Golden Age of Hai": Don and Alice Gibbons and their family worked among the Damal people and others in Papua for over forty years, beginning in 1953. Alice wrote two books about their ministry there, *The People Time Forgot* and *Where the Earth Ends*. The conversion of the Damal people in huge numbers, beginning with Nogom and Chief Den, occurred in 1957, less than a year after Don had first arrived in their midst. (Nogom's real name was Nogombunime.)

Many heroes aren't named in this book. Among them are the pilots who faithfully flew the airplanes for the missionaries after they cleared land for the airstrips. These pilots, most of whom were with Mission Aviation

Fellowship, served missionaries in several different mission organizations.

Chapter 4 "Power Pieces": Tom and Frances Bozeman and their family worked among the Grand Valley Dani tribe for many years, beginning in 1956. The story of Hilitu (which I read in *Cannibal Valley*, by Russell Hitt) took place around that time.

Chapter 5 "Nabelan Kabelan?": Gordon and Peggy Larson and their family ministered among the Western Danis and others from 1956 to 1992. The story of Lalok and his clan happened within a year of the conversion of the Damals. (Lalok's real name was Obalalok.)

Chapter 6 "Jabonep the Witness Man": Henry and Bernice Young and their family worked among the Pyramid Danis beginning in 1956. The story of Jabonep occurred in 1959, after Henry's preaching had been falling on deaf ears for three years.

Chapter 7 "Burning the Power Pieces": Jim and Deloris Sunda and their family worked among the Pyramid Danis for 39 years. The burning at Pyramid happened shortly after Jabonep's preaching.

Chapter 8 "Words of Life!": David Martin, later with his wife Margy and their children, worked with the Toli Valley Dani from 1959 to 1980, and has since made regular trips back to encourage the Dani pastors.

In every country I research, I see the fingerprints of Gospel Recordings (now called Global Recordings). This is the ingenious and mammoth vision, begun in 1939 by Joy Ridderhof, of recording the glorious Good News told by native speakers, in as many languages as possible around the world. Don and Eunice Richter recorded in Papua in 1959, but Don served the Lord with Gospel Recordings from 1952 to 1969, in various places throughout the world. They did their part to accomplish the goal of recording the life-changing gospel of Jesus Christ in—so far—over five thousand languages. (Jagomi's real name is Mejagome. In some sources, the Toli Valley is called the Swart Valley.)

Chapter 9 "I Saw You in My Dream": Dave and Esther Scovill and their family worked among the Danis of the Baliem Valley beginning in 1960 to 1980, and then served in other capacities for over twenty more years. The story of Wat is found in Dave's book, *The Amazing Danis*. (Wat's real name is Wa'lumbuk.)

Chapters 10-11 "Sprinkling Cool Water" and "Peace Child": For Don and Carol Richardson, July 14, 2012 marked the fiftieth anniversary of their ride in a dugout canoe to take the gospel to the Sawi people of Papua. Don has written many books, one of which, *Eternity in Their Hearts*, inspired me thirty years ago to want to someday write books of missionary stories. Another of his books, *Peace Child*, tells the story that is recounted in these chapters.

Chapter 12 "Changes in Church": John and Helen Dekker and their family worked among the Danis of the

Toli Valley from 1960 to 1981. John chronicles their work in *Torches of Joy*, which showed such a cute picture of their family, especially their son Ted, that I wrote about it on my blog. (Rigwi's real name was Mbyrigwe. His story is told in *An Hour to the Stone Age* by Shirley Horne.)

Chapter 13 "The Spirit Who Loves": After working among the Danis for two years, Phil and Phyliss Masters and their family took the gospel to the Kimyal people in 1963. After Phil was killed by the Yali tribe in 1968, Phyliss left the area, but continued to serve God in other ways. When she returned to the Kimyal tribe in 2010 for the dedication of their New Testament, a Yali tribesman sought her out. He had recently read *Lords of the Earth*, a book by Don Richardson that described his own tribe. In reading that book, he discovered that his own people had been responsible for the death of Phyliss's husband, so he wanted personally to offer apologies, thanks, and love from his tribe.

Several other missionaries, including Orin and Rosa Kidd, who came in 1977, continued the teaching that Phil and Phyliss had begun, and continued to help with the Bible translation, even after returning to the United States.

Chapter 14 "Bad Legs Woman": Elinor Young served among the Kimyal people, especially working on the translation of the New Testament, beginning in 1973, and at the time of Chapter 14, was the only missionary living among the Kimyals. In 1991, post-polio syndrome forced Elinor to leave Papua and return to her home in Washington state, where she continues to write and serve her Savior.

Chapter 15 "Bible Party": The hidden hero Siud served as the catalyst for this book. I continue to marvel that such a spiritual tower in the mighty work of God stands only four feet eight inches tall. If you haven't yet seen the video, you can search online for "Kimyal Tribe New Testament" and rejoice with us that the Word of God is going forth in power over all the world.

THINKING FURTHER

CHAPTER 1 – DISCOVERY

"Some sat in darkness and in the shadow of death, prisoners in affliction and in irons." Psalm 107: 10

Imagine that you heard that an entirely new group of people had just been discovered. What would be your first thoughts? For many Christians, their first thoughts were "Those people need the gospel of Jesus Christ!" For many others, their first thoughts were, "We should leave them alone. They're happy the way they are." What do you think? Do you think the gospel might change their lives too much, or change their lives in a wrong way?

CHAPTER 2 – ACROSS THE WORLD

"And he said to them, 'Go into all the world and proclaim the gospel to the whole creation.'" Mark 16:15

Mark 16:15 is called the "Great Commission." These are words Jesus spoke to his disciples just before He went back into heaven. Can you think of any people in the Bible who spent their lives and energy taking the gospel to as many people as possible? Do you know of any other people in history who did the same? What are some reasons you could tell from this chapter that these tribal people needed the gospel of Jesus Christ?

CHAPTER 3 – THE GOLDEN AGE OF HAI

"Jesus said to her, 'Everyone who drinks of this water will be thirsty again, but whoever drinks of the water that I will give him shall never thirst; but the water that I will give him will become in him a well of water springing up to eternal life.'" John 4:13-14

How did Den know to be waiting for some important words about eternal life? How did Den's father's dream seem to be about Jesus? Acts, chapter 10, tells of a man named Cornelius who was told by God in a vision to call for a man named Peter to come. Read that story, and discuss how his story is similar to the story of Den's father.

CHAPTER 4 – POWER PIECES

"For God gave us a spirit not of fear, but of power and love and self-control."
2 Timothy 1:7

Hilitu's power pieces had been specially dedicated to the spirits. Do you think that destroying them made Hilitu a Christian? Why was it important that he destroy them?

CHAPTER 5 – NABELAN KABELAN?

"How then will they call on him in whom they have not believed? And how are they to believe in him of whom they have never heard? And how are they to hear without someone preaching?" Romans 10:14

Describe the legend of nabelan kabelan. Do you think it's true? How could the missionaries use it to teach the gospel? Why do you think Lalok and other Papuans took so long to receive the truth of Jesus, even after they thought it might be true? Do you think they were wise to do that?

CHAPTER 6 – JABONED THE WITNESS MAN

"Sing to the LORD, all the earth! Tell of his salvation from day to day. Declare his glory among the nations, his marvelous works among all the peoples!"
1 Chronicles 16:23-24

Henry Young had been preaching to the people of Pyramid Valley for three years. Why hadn't they listened to him? What made the difference in reaching them with the gospel?

CHAPTER 7 - BURNING THE POWER PIECES

"And a number of those who had practiced magic arts brought their books together and burned them in the sight of all." Acts 19:19

Acts 19:11-20 tells the story of a great work of God in Ephesus, with a burning at the end. Explain why it was important to burn some things that were worth a lot of money. Why did the Papuan people treat it like a celebration?

CHAPTER 8 - WORDS OF LIFE!

"Truly, truly, I say to you, whoever hears my word and believes him who sent me has eternal life. He does not come into judgment, but has passed from death to life." John 5:24

The missionaries in Papua taught stories from the Old Testament, beginning with Creation. Why was it important to teach those stories? Name some Old Testament stories that could give a picture of the sacrifice of Jesus Christ.

CHAPTER 9 - I SAW YOU IN MY DREAM

"The field is the world, and the good seed is the sons of the kingdom. The weeds are the sons of the evil one." Matthew 13:38

In Matthew 13: 24-30 Jesus tells the parable of the wheat and the weeds. In verses 36-43 He explains that parable. How do you think the Papuan people would understand this parable? What do you think they might have talked about around their fires after hearing it?

CHAPTER 10 – SPRINKLING COOL WATER

"Put on the whole armor of God, that you may be able to stand against the schemes of the devil." Ephesians 6:11

Read about God's armor in Ephesians 6:11-19. Don and Carol Richardson were fighting a spiritual battle. What are some of the things God had given them to fight that battle? How did they show that they had the shield of faith?

CHAPTER 11 – PEACE CHILD

"For to us a child is born, to us a son is given; and the government shall be upon his shoulder, and his name shall be called Wonderful Counselor, Mighty God, Everlasting Father, Prince of Peace." Isaiah 9:6

Why did this Bible verse become important in Don Richardson's ministry with the Sawi? What did they come to understand that they hadn't understood before?

CHAPTER 12 – CHANGES IN CHURCH

"Therefore, if anyone is in Christ, he is a new creation. The old has passed away; behold, the new has come." 2 Corinthians 5:17

Name some of the ways the Papuan people changed as they began to learn more of the ways of God. What people in the Bible changed as the Holy Spirit transformed their lives?

CHAPTER 13 – THE SPIRIT WHO LOVES

"I pray that you will be able to know the love of Christ that surpasses knowledge, that you may be filled with all the fullness of God." Ephesians 3:19

One of the truths that astonished the Papuan people was that there was a Spirit who loves. How do you think Siud had already thought about this? How did Ephesians 3:19 begin to come true in his life?

CHAPTER 14 – BAD LEGS WOMAN

"Listen to Me, O islands, and pay attention, you peoples from afar. The LORD called me from the womb; from the body of my mother He named me. He made my mouth like a sharp sword; in the shadow of his hand he hid me; he made me a polished arrow; in his quiver he hid me away. And he said to me, 'You are my servant ... in whom I will be glorified.'" Isaiah 49:1-3

Elinor had a dream, even when she was young. Was this dream the same as God's plan for her? How can you be sure that it's a good thing to move forward with your dream? Why do you think some people thought that Elinor couldn't be a missionary? Why did Elinor think differently? What are some ways the Kimyal people showed Elinor that her handicap was a blessing to them?

CHAPTER 15 – BIBLE PARTY

"And let us not grow weary of doing good, for in due season we will reap, if we do not give up." Galatians 6:9

Do you think there were times when Rosa and others might have felt like giving up? Why? Can you think of a time in the Bible when someone might have felt like giving up? What does the Lord promise for those who don't give up when they're working for His glory?

CHRISTIAN FOCUS PUBLICATIONS

Christian Focus | Christian Heritage | CF4K | Mentor

Christian Focus Publications publishes books for adults and children under its four main imprints: Christian Focus, CF4K, Mentor and Christian Heritage. Our books reflect our conviction that God's Word is reliable and Jesus is the way to know him, and live for ever with him.

Our children's publication list includes a Sunday School curriculum that covers pre-school to early teens, and puzzle and activity books. We also publish personal and family devotional titles, biographies and inspirational stories that children will love.

If you are looking for quality Bible teaching for children then we have an excellent range of Bible stories and age-specific theological books.

From pre-school board books to teenage apologetics, we have it covered!

**Find us at our web page:
www.christianfocus.com**

CF4 •K
*Because you're never
too young to know Jesus*